T0003972

YOU'RE NOT FINISHED YET

100 Devotions for Building Strength
and Faith for Your Journey

CHRISTINE CAINE

THOMAS NELSON
Since 1798

You're Not Finished Yet

© 2023 Caso Writing, LLC

Some text in this book has been drawn from the following books: *Unexpected: Leave Fear Behind, Move Forward in Faith, Embrace the Adventure* (Zondervan), *Unashamed: Drop the Baggage, Pick Up Your Freedom, Fulfill Your Destiny* (Zondervan), *Undaunted: Daring to Do What God Calls You to Do* (Zondervan), *How Did I Get Here?: Finding Your Way Back to God When Everything Is Pulling You Away* (Thomas Nelson), and *20/20 Seen. Chosen. Sent.* (Lifeway).

Published in Nashville, Tennessee, by Thomas Nelson. Thomas Nelson is a registered trademark of HarperCollins Christian Publishing, Inc.

Published in association with Yates & Yates, www.yates2.com.

Thomas Nelson titles may be purchased in bulk for educational, business, fundraising, or sales promotional use. For information, please email SpecialMarkets@ThomasNelson.com.

Unless otherwise noted, Scripture quotations are from the Christian Standard Bible. Copyright © 2017 by Holman Bible Publishers. Used by permission. Christian Standard Bible® and CSB® are federally registered trademarks of Holman Bible Publishers, all rights reserved.

Scripture quotations marked AMPC are taken from the Amplified® Bible (AMPC). Copyright © 1954, 1958, 1962, 1964, 1965, 1987 by The Lockman Foundation. Used by permission. www.Lockman.org.

Scripture quotations marked ESV are taken from the ESV® Bible (The Holy Bible, English Standard Version®). Copyright © 2001 by Crossway, a publishing ministry of Good News Publishers. Used by permission. All rights reserved.

Scripture quotations marked KJV are taken from the King James Version. Public domain.

Scripture quotations marked NIV are taken from the Holy Bible, New International Version®, NIV®. Copyright © 1973, 1978, 1984, 2011 by Biblica, Inc.® Used by permission of Zondervan. All rights reserved worldwide. www.zondervan.com. The "NIV" and "New International Version" are trademarks registered in the United States Patent and Trademark Office by Biblica, Inc.®

Scripture quotations marked NKJV are taken from the New King James Version®. Copyright © 1982 by Thomas Nelson. Used by permission. All rights reserved.

Any internet addresses, phone numbers, or company or product information printed in this book are offered as a resource and are not intended in any way to be or to imply an endorsement by Thomas Nelson, nor does Thomas Nelson vouch for the existence, content, or services of these sites, phone numbers, companies, or products beyond the life of this book.

ISBN 978-1-4002-3321-2 (audiobook)
ISBN 978-1-4002-3320-5 (eBook)
ISBN 978-1-4002-3318-2 (HC)

Printed in India

23 24 25 26 27 REP 10 9 8 7 6 5 4 3 2 1

To everyone who's in the middle.

CONTENTS

Introduction: Faith and Strength for the Messy Middle vi

PART 1: WALKING EVERYWHERE WITH JESUS 1

PART 2: PEACE: HIS PRESENCE IN OUR MINDS 53

PART 3: RUNNING OUR RACE WITH PERSEVERANCE . . 105

PART 4: PATIENCE: OUR STRENGTH IN THE WAITING . . 157

Notes 208

Acknowledgments 211

About the Author 213

INTRODUCTION

Faith and Strength for

the Messy Middle

You have plantar fasciitis, Ms. Caine, and if you want to keep hiking, then you'll need to do exactly as I say."

Listening to the podiatrist, whom I'd known for less than an hour, I needed no convincing that I was in trouble. If he knew the way forward, I was all in. I had been increasingly unable to bear weight on my foot, especially in the mornings when I got out of bed. Never had I felt such stabbing pain in my heel the minute it hit the floor. I was willing to do whatever it took to get out of pain and to keep hiking mountain trails—something I never thought I'd feel so passionate about.

What started as a way to get out of the house and see the great outdoors in 2020 had grown into something God used to teach me, train me, and build His endurance in me. For a year my friend Dawn and I had trekked every trail we could find in Southern California. Then, when all the odds were against us, in 2021, we won a lottery drawing to climb Mount Whitney, the tallest mountain in the contiguous United States, standing at 14,505 feet. It was then that I began intentionally training so I could manage the seventeen-hour climb along with the elevation changes.

But with all the training came injuries, first to my hip, which landed me in repeated appointments with physical therapy, and then to my foot. I had been putting extra pressure on myself, and it had been brutal, but I was committed. Still, I had to take care of my body if I wanted to keep going.

"Plantar fasciitis is when the thick band of tissue connecting the bottom of your heel to your toes becomes inflamed," the doctor went on to explain, pointing his pen to a diagram on the wall showing all the bones and tendons in my foot. "You can keep hiking, but you'll need to get an orthotic insert for your shoes."

As he went on trying to encourage me but help me understand the significance of my injury and why I would have to care for it, all I could focus on was that diagram . . . and that long stretch of tissue running from my heel to my toes, all the way down the middle of my foot.

Not intending to zone out on valuable information, I couldn't help but begin to think, *Why is it that what's in the middle of everything is the most important part? Why is the middle of everything the hardest part? Why can't we go from the beginning of anything and jump to the end, skipping the middle altogether?*

Maybe that's just how my mind works, jumping all around and connecting what doesn't seem to be connected, particularly when I'm supposed to be listening intently. I tend to look beyond the obvious much of the time. And today, I was focused on the middle—of my foot . . . and of everything else—because somehow the significance of the middle is what captured my attention. Even when I left the doctor's office, I couldn't stop thinking about the significance of the middle.

The middle is that place you reach when you're not where you were, but you're not where you're going, and you have to keep going to get where you're going. Did you catch all that? It's when the novelty has worn off. It's when life gets hard. It's where you may be tempted to simply stop. But you can't . . . because you're not finished yet.

I remember feeling this way many times in my ministry life. When it was hard. When it felt unbearable. When all that my heart and soul wanted to do was quit. Decades later, God's still using me because I'm still here. Because I found a way to keep going through the middle, particularly all the mini-middles along the way.

Somehow, continuing to climb mountains and work through hip-flexor pain and heel pain felt much the same—even when every ounce of my fifty-seven-year-old body reminded me I had plenty of reasons to quit. Despite it all, I wanted to keep going. I wanted to make it through the middle.

You'll be relieved to know that I read some research on my condition that was a bit more scientific than my musings, but I do believe I was on to something. Did you know that when serious runners train for a race, they train for the middle? Understandably, the middle of any race is the hardest part. It's where a runner begins to run out of energy, strength, and the mental focus to keep going. Whether they're a sprinter or a distance runner, if they don't make it through the middle, they won't make it across the finish line. It sounds so simple, but it requires strategic training to succeed because the middle is *hard*. You want to quit, you're not sure how you can keep going, but you know you're not finished yet.

From a spiritual perspective, isn't the middle what we're in training for during much of our lives? Think of it this way: we're born one day, spiritually speaking, and then we begin this race, which is our journey in Christ on this earth, all in hopes of crossing the finish line someday and hearing that we did a good job with the race we ran.[1] That might be an oversimplification, but it sums up our lives really well, doesn't it?

Someday, when I finish my race, I want to be able to say like the apostle Paul, "I have fought the good fight, I have finished the race, I have kept the faith."[2] But to do that, I first have to get through the middle.

To get through the middle—of everything—you will need endurance. The writer of Hebrews wrote, "You have need of endurance, so that when you have done the will of God you may receive what is promised."[3]

Endurance is formally defined as "the ability or strength to continue despite fatigue, stress or adverse conditions."[4] It's the capacity to bear up under difficult circumstances. The power to withstand pain or hardships. It's a hopeful fortitude that perseveres to the end. In the original Greek language of the New Testament, it is *hupomone*, a compound word that translates "to remain under."[5] It is a quality built by remaining under pressure—something our natural inclination wants to run away from—and it seems to hit us the hardest in the middle.

In the middle of our friendships.
In the middle of our dating relationships.
In the middle of our marriages.
In the middle of our parenting.
In the middle of our education.
In the middle of building our careers.
In the middle of an illness.
In the middle of a court case.
In the middle of a transition.
In the middle of something we're hoping and praying will happen.
In the middle of waiting on answers.

In the middle of anything is where it's the most tedious, the most difficult, and utterly wearisome. It's where we're most challenged, isn't it? It's where all we want to do is quit. But if we will build endurance, that strength the writer of Hebrews told us we would need, if we will train ourselves from the Word of God, and by the power of the Holy Spirit, we will have the wherewithal to make it through the middle. Not just one middle but every middle we will ever live through.

Are you in a middle? Then this devotional is for you. Because every day is a dose of the endurance you will need to get through the middle. If you haven't read *Resilient Hope*, get it too. And when my next devotional is released, add it to your must-reads because it's going to share glimmers of the victory you'll receive when you finish this hard but glorious race. Although I recommend you start with *Resilient Hope,* these devotional books are written so you can start where you like and when you like. Together, the devotions will help you build the endurance you need to run every day of your race on mission, and after having done the will of God, cross the finish line.

Love you so much,

Chris Caine

PART 1

WALKING EVERYWHERE WITH JESUS

Of all the paths you take in life, make sure a few of them are dirt.

JOHN MUIR

1 WALK IN JESUS

So then, just as you have received Christ Jesus as Lord, continue to walk in him.

COLOSSIANS 2:6

I do my best to love all God's creatures, but I have to admit, I do not like snakes. I can't stand them. I'll go so far as to say I hate them. And yes, I understand I'm supposed to love, not hate, which includes God's creatures. But I seriously doubt Adam and Eve loved them after they left the garden. Have you ever thought about that?

What I especially hate about them is the way they make my heart skip a beat when I see them. It's so unnerving. I feel like I have to expend all this extra energy to calm myself down, get my head back in the right space, and survive a mild heart attack. I'm a bit dramatic, I know, but snakes bring out the worst in me. Living in Southern California, I see way too many of them, most often in the summer. It's as though they target me. On three weekend hikes in a row, as I was nearing the summit, a fellow hiker who had made it to the top and was heading back down felt compelled to tell me, "Be careful, there's a huge rattlesnake up ahead." Why? I'm so much better not knowing. One minute I'm starting to feel thrilled that I'm almost to the highest point, and the next, I'm not sure I can go one more step. I'm frozen from the idea of encountering a snake.

It's surprising how sometimes the hike up a mountain is beautiful and all I can focus on is how amazing it is. But sometimes it's terrifying, like when I encounter a snake—or at least think I will. Either way, what I won't do is stop walking—and including others along the way.

I have found that when I hike with my friend Dawn, I walk better than I ever would on my own. When I walk with her, because she's such an experienced hiker, she's able to point out things I might miss. She sees things I don't see. A kind of flower. An ancient tree. A chipmunk. A bird. A deer. And yes, a snake curled up under the brush. She hears things I would never hear, like the near-silent sound of a mountain lion pacing alongside the trail, as curious about us as we are about him. From all my walks with Dawn, I have noticed how we fall into a familiar cadence. We stay in step. And not just physically. We've grown in our friendship. In our willingness to share. A camaraderie has developed. We look out for each other, and neither of us wants the other to miss anything. Walking together has helped us both grow stronger, and not just on the trail. We've grown spiritually, increasing in our endurance.

I can't help but think this is what Jesus wants for us as we walk in Him. Paul wrote that just as we have received Jesus as our Lord, we are to continue walking in Him. When we walk in Jesus, we see things we might not otherwise see. We hear things we might not otherwise hear. He points things out He doesn't want us to miss. And there's an intimacy that grows. A camaraderie that develops. An endurance we can't build any other way.

Jesus, help me continue walking in You, staying in step with You. I want to see what You see, hear what You hear, and grow closer to You. I love You. In Your name, amen.

2 KEEP IT SIMPLE

Mankind, he has told each of you what is good and what it is the LORD requires of you: to act justly, to love faithfulness, and to walk humbly with your God.

MICAH 6:8

When Nick and I married and merged our worlds, he said to me, "We're going to keep it simple. Evangelism will always be a part of everything we do. We'll reach the lost. We'll keep loving God, and we'll keep loving people." More than two decades later, we're still enduring in faith and going strong. And when it starts to get complicated in my head, Nick has been faithful to remind us both to keep it simple.

In the years we've worked at this, I've come to think one of my favorite things about God is that He never overcomplicates things. We, on the other hand, in our humanity, are brilliant at overcomplicating most everything. That includes how we see God and how we live for Him on this earth. If only we would just take God at face value, read His Word, and follow His instructions. I think if we would, it would all be pretty simple, right? Despite how hard we can make it, Christianity is not complex. I admit that it's not always easy, but it's not complex. I like how the prophet Micah simplified it in today's verse. He told us exactly what God requires of us, and it's three simple things: act justly, love faithfulness, and walk humbly.

From what this verse says, God wants us walking this side of eternity. He's talking about an engagement in life—in society. He doesn't want us to run ahead of Him. He doesn't want us to stand behind Him. Or sit in place. He wants us walking with Him, building endurance with Him. I find it intentional that God uses the word *walk*, because walking demonstrates intimacy with Him. It denotes a proximity to Him. It's more than just learning about Him; it's actually being with Him and walking humbly with Him.

When we walk humbly with God, we see what He sees, we do what He does, we care for what He cares for. Our hearts begin to change, our eyes open to injustice, and we want to do something about it. We don't want to miss a moment of being in step with Him, so we want to remain faithful, even when it's hard.

I want my heart to beat for what God's heart beats for, don't you? I have found that I can do this only when I walk intimately with Him. When I walk humbly with Him. When I'm willing to learn, to grow, to change. The minute I separate myself from walking with God, from having time in His Word each day, from being planted in a church, from being connected with my Christian friends, from worshiping Him and praying and talking with Him, my heart shifts. And I find myself not loving faithfulness as much or not acting justly as often.

Let's not overcomplicate it. Let's do like Micah said: let's act justly, love faithfulness, and walk humbly. It's not easy to do, but it is simple.

Father, when my mind gets to spinning and overcomplicating my walk, help me keep it simple. To do acts of justice, to love mercy, and to walk humbly with You. In Jesus' name, amen.

3 HOW BIG GOD IS

Moses was a very humble man, more so than anyone on the face of the earth.
NUMBERS 12:3

When I read this verse, I can't help but think of all that Moses did. He was the man who led the Israelites out of captivity in Egypt, held the rod through which God parted the Red Sea, met with God on the mountaintop, carried the actual tablets of the Ten Commandments—though he later smashed them in a moment of anger—and even saw the back of God when he asked to see His glory. This man who knew God, who revered God, who got as close to God as he could get and still live was said to be humbler than anyone who walked the face of the earth. When I read this in Scripture, I tend to think that when we get that up close and personal with God, we truly understand that God is God, and we are not. We know the difference. And therein lies the key to understanding true humility.

Sometimes, in our effort to put the Word into practice, I think we mistakenly confuse humility with ideas of low self-esteem or thinking less of oneself. But being humble is not about putting ourselves down or projecting ourselves as less than we are or as knowing less than we do. Being humble is about recognizing how big God is. It is about having a right view of ourselves in relationship to Him. It is about living with an awareness that God is God, and we are not. It's about knowing who we are in Him: children of the King.[6] Filled with the same Spirit that raised Jesus from the dead.[7] It is about living in a divine tension of acknowledging that outside of God I can do nothing, but in Christ I can do all things.[8]

Do you see the difference? I want to walk humbly with my God. I want to be humble in everything I do. Honoring God. Acknowledging God. Trusting God. Walking with Him daily. Dependent on Him in every moment. Aware of how big He is and how it's only in Him that I can be all He's created me to be and fulfill all the purpose He has for me. I can endure with strength in faith until I step into eternity. Putting myself down will never achieve any of that.

The next time you start to put yourself down, catch yourself. Turn your thoughts to God and how big He is. Think of all you are in Him, of all you can do in Him. Find verses that speak of this and personalize them, saying them aloud to yourself and to God in that moment. It's one more way we can continue to be transformed so we see ourselves the way He does, as someone created in His image. It's one more way we can remind ourselves how big God is.

Heavenly Father, help me understand true humility and walk in it today. Help me see how big You are in every circumstance in my life. In Jesus' name, amen.

4 CREATED TO MOVE FORWARD

Brothers and sisters, I do not consider myself to have taken hold of it. But one thing I do: Forgetting what is behind and reaching forward to what is ahead.
PHILIPPIANS 3:13

The Australian coat of arms depicts a very insightful image, one that I hold dear since I was born and raised in Australia and because it speaks volumes to me personally. There are two animals portrayed holding up a shield—the red kangaroo and the emu. They were chosen not only because they are indigenous to Australia but also because they were created to move forward.

The emu, a large, nonflying bird slightly smaller than its cousin the ostrich, is known for its speed, covering as much as nine feet in a single step when running full throttle. It is the only bird with calf muscles—much like a human. Nonetheless, it can't walk backward. It can only move forward.

The red kangaroo—like all kangaroos—moves by a hopping motion called saltation, which literally means "to leap." They push off with both of their large feet simultaneously and use their tails for balance. The combination of their muscular legs, big feet, and tails helps the kangaroos move forward effectively. But again, they can only move forward—not backward.[9]

When I think of them, and the fact they are creatures God made that cannot walk backward, I can't help but think of us—people made in the image of God, another marvel of creation designed to move the same way. I understand that we need to step back from time to time and remember the past so we can move forward, and life sometimes hits us and we feel like we have gone backward, but God is faithful to pick us up and keep us moving forward. We are all on journeys no matter where we are. In some seasons we move forward quickly, and in others we move more slowly, but overall, we keep pressing on. Though we might pause and look to the past, we don't want to get stuck in the past, right? How often have we allowed a season of disappointment, hurt, rejection, offense, or fear to stop us from moving forward? Today is a good day to take the hand of Jesus and, like the emu and the red kangaroo, take the next step forward.

Let's take Paul's advice to the Philippians, forgetting what is behind and reaching forward to what is ahead. We can't change the past. Not one bit. But we can affect our future. We can keep enduring in faith, reaching for all that God has planned for us. We can keep moving in the only direction we were created to move.

The emu. The red kangaroo. And you. All created to move forward. Never backward. Let's be who God created us to be so we can do all that He's called us to do!

Heavenly Father, thank You that even in nature You give us examples. You give us insight. Help us move the way You created us to move—forward, and never backward. In Jesus' name, amen.

5 TIME TO TAKE GROUND

"I have given you every place where the sole of your foot treads, just as I promised Moses. Your territory will be from the wilderness and Lebanon to the great river, the Euphrates River—all the land of the Hittites—and west to the Mediterranean Sea."

JOSHUA 1:3-4

would love to say that when I first gave my heart fully to the Lord, I instantly changed and began to walk and talk like a Christian. That I immediately transformed into having all the character that Jesus displayed for us when He walked the earth. That all the fruit of the Spirit just sprouted and was hanging off me. That every time I opened my mouth I sounded like a glorified saint. If only!

When I yielded all of me to all of Him, I had no idea how to live like a Christian. Yes, I had been raised in church with awareness of who Jesus was, but I didn't know Him. I only knew about Him. When I did meet Him, my heart absolutely, totally changed, but it took time before the rest of me caught on. (And I still have a long way to go.) I was eager to learn, often leaning forward in my chair on a Sunday, but everything was new to me. The way people freely worshiped. The way they opened Bibles and followed along with the pastor. The way people greeted me and made me feel so welcome. I had never known anything like that. But the more I kept going, the more I began to learn what the Bible said and how to apply it to my life.

Still, I had to do the work of changing. Nothing was automatic. It was just like what God instructed the children of Israel in today's verse. God promised to them the land everywhere their feet would tread, but they still had to do the treading. They had to start moving forward, putting one foot in front of the other, confronting all the obstacles they encountered along the way, to possess what God had already given them—the promised land.

When I read, "I have given you every place where the sole of your foot treads," I understand a divine tension between the sovereignty of God and the free will of man. God has done it all, and given it all to us, but to experience the joy of partnering with Him and seeing His will come to pass, we have to get to treading. I like to say it this way: We have to get out there and take some ground, just like the children of Israel did. The ground does not automatically fall into our laps; we have to go to it—and that requires effort, resilience, tenacity, courage, and strength. It will not happen if we spend our lives here on earth binge-watching the latest series.

Since you gave your life to Jesus, have you continued taking ground in your life? Have you continued enduring in faith? Or have you gotten bogged down somewhere along the way? If you have, it's time to get up and start putting one foot in front of the other. It's time to take some ground.

Heavenly Father, help me walk in all the promises You have given to me. Show me where I've stopped treading and help me start putting one foot in front of the other, in You. In Jesus' name, amen.

6 THE BEST PLACE

I know how to make do with little, and I know how to make do with a lot. In any and all circumstances I have learned the secret of being content—whether well fed or hungry, whether in abundance or in need.

PHILIPPIANS 4:12

When I first started playing golf, I wanted so badly to just get on the course, play eighteen holes, and relish being a great golfer. But that was not how it was going to happen. I had to work at it from the very start. There was so much to learn. I first had to study how the game is played. Then I had to learn how to hold a club, how to swing, what each club is used for, and how to play each hole. There was nothing about it that I had ever done before. I'm more the girl who'd rather be hiking mountains or walking on the beach, not swinging at a ball all over a perfectly manicured lawn. But I wanted to learn.

In everything I've wanted to do, I'm not sure anything has come without effort. Whether it was playing sports, growing spiritually, parenting our girls, being married, or starting an initiative, I've had to learn how to do it. Perhaps that's why today's verse means so much to me. Paul wrote that he had learned the secret of being content. It wasn't something he automatically knew how to do or something that came upon him when he gave his life to God. It was something he learned. To learn means to gain knowledge or understanding or skill by study, instruction, or experience.[10]

What is equally powerful is that Paul didn't just learn how to be content; we know from his other writings that he pressed on, he reached forward, he strained for more. He said he would keep going as long as he could, doing the work of Christ.[11] How could he say he learned to be content and yet acknowledge that he was never going to stop going for more?

Because his contentment was in Christ. Whatever circumstance Paul was in, he had Jesus. He did not find his contentment in the next achievement or accolade; he found it in Christ. So much of our spiritual walk here on earth is about getting us to a place where we learn to be content in Christ while we are on our way to inheriting His promises for our lives. Yes, we may be single and want to be married, but we are learning to be content. We may be changing diapers and want to build a business, but we are learning to be content. We may be married, and our marriage isn't where we want it to be, but we are learning to be content. Learning is what produces endurance, and endurance is what we need to finish our race. Are you learning to be content? In any and all circumstances? I hope so, because it's the best place we can be.

Jesus, help me learn how to be content but not satisfied. To be at peace where I am while always reaching for more of You and who You are, and for more of who You want me to be. In Your name, amen.

7 THE POSTURE
OF HUMILITY

He [Jesus] humbled himself by becoming obedient to the point of death—even to death on a cross.

PHILIPPIANS 2:8

_____

When I hear myself telling my girls to sit up straight or to walk with their shoulders back, I sometimes feel like I can hear my mother's voice because I sound just like she did.

"Christina," she would say, "mind your posture. Don't slouch like that. Sit up." When she would remind me, I would get so frustrated because I preferred to slouch. Even when she explained why I needed to sit up straight, I found it so much more comfortable not to. Giving in to gravity is always easier than working against it, right? It's more convenient to hunch our shoulders over the table at dinner or to lean over our desks at work. And if you're like me, once I start eating or working, the last thing I'm thinking about is my posture. But alas, Mum was right. She knew that the older I grew, the more I would care, and that good habits are much easier to form when we're young. So, like Mum, I do my best to keep my girls mindful of their posture, but I have taken it a step further.

Just as much as I've worked to remind our girls about their physical posture, of how they are to walk physically, I've done my best to teach them about their spiritual posture, of how they are to walk spiritually. It's something Jesus demonstrated for us that I believe we're to learn from and imitate. I believe it makes us strong and able to endure in our Christian walk.

Scripture tells us that Jesus walked humbly. That was His posture. He humbled Himself by coming to serve—to the point of death, Paul said. Jesus was submitted to God, His humility grounded in the character of God. It was a virtue.[12]

As Christ-followers, we're to walk in the same way. But how do we do that? In a world full of chaos, division, pain, and suffering, I would think there ought to be something different in the way that we act and the way we speak. Our world needs love. Joy. Peace. Kindness. If we are going to walk humbly, then we need to be fueled by the Spirit of God and the Word of God. We need our words, actions, even social media posts to reflect the heart of Jesus. A posture of humility is a posture of learning. Of listening. Of understanding that not everyone's experience is like my experience. It's a posture of unifying people and situations— and building bridges. It's a posture of wanting to be part of the solution in every circumstance.

So, how is your posture? Are you walking humbly with God? If you're like me, you're aware that you can always do better. Let's move forward in this together today as we prefer others over ourselves, as we give them deference in situations and conversations, as we work to encourage one another. Let's walk, humbling ourselves even more.

Jesus, please help me consciously walk humbly today. Help me put others first and consider their perspectives and feelings before I speak, act, or post. In Your name, amen.

8 TAKE A DIFFERENT ROUTE

"Whoever drinks from the water that I will give him will never get thirsty again. In fact, the water I will give him will become a well of water springing up in him for eternal life."

JOHN 4:14

When Jesus spoke these words, He was having a conversation with a woman at a well outside a town in Samaria. He was traveling from Judea in the south to Galilee in the north when He chose to pass through the region. Normally, Jewish travelers chose a route around Samaria to avoid contact with the Samaritans because Jews considered them to be racially impure and unworthy of fellowship—and God's favor.

But not Jesus. He took the direct route, causing Him to encounter the woman. Having walked a great distance, He was resting beside the well when she came to draw water. I imagine He was hot, weary, and maybe even hungry from His journey. We know He was thirsty, because He asked her for a drink; but rather than grant His request right away, she questioned Him. Why would a Jew ask her, a Samaritan woman, for a drink? Not only was it odd for Jesus to talk to a Samaritan, but it was also equally uncommon for someone like Him to strike up a conversation with a woman—who was alone—and she knew it.

But Jesus had something for her. When He responded, He offered her living water—the kind that could quench her thirst for eternity. He told her things about herself that He could have only known by the Spirit. Then, He went on to reveal Himself for the first time as the Messiah. To her. A Samaritan woman. The more He talked, the more she was transformed. Because she was so moved, she ran to tell the people in her village, and many came to believe just as she had—all because Jesus took a different route on His way to a familiar place.

When was the last time you took a different route on your way to a familiar place? To work, school, or shopping? When did you last sit in a different seat at church? Did you encounter someone you might not have met otherwise? Did it feel like a divine appointment?

I have found that we might have to walk through some places we normally wouldn't to reach who God has waiting for us. And it most likely won't happen at a convenient time. In fact, I bet it will happen when we most want to race home, take a break, get all our errands done, or be left completely alone. But if we ever give in to that nudging of the Holy Spirit and help someone when it is anything but convenient, we will know the reward and value of sharing the enduring life of faith Jesus has given us. The life that began when we accepted His invitation to drink His living water.

As we walk through today, let's be willing to take a different route—to go out of our way. Let's live expectant, ready to embrace the people and divine appointments waiting for us.

Jesus, please lead me and guide me to divine appointments. Help me remember to rest in the detours and trust You along the way. Help me see the people in my path. In Your name, amen.

9 OUT OF OPTIONS

Now four men with a skin disease were at the entrance to the city gate. They said to each other, "Why just sit here until we die? If we say, 'Let's go into the city,' we will die there because the famine is in the city, but if we sit here, we will also die. So now, come on. Let's surrender to the Arameans' camp. If they let us live, we will live; if they kill us, we will die."

2 KINGS 7:3–4

In ancient times, it didn't get much worse than being a leper. They were the complete outcasts of society, feared and loathed on account of the perceived threat of contagion. More than that, leprosy was considered by many to be a divine curse on man. As we listen in on the conversation in today's verses, four lepers were sitting outside the gate of the city, and it's hard to miss how desperate they were. Debating among themselves, they discussed how if they stayed at the city gate, they would die. If they went into the city, because there was such a great famine happening at the time, they would die. And even if they took their best option, to go to the Arameans' camp, they might die there too. Then again, there was a chance the Arameans might let them live. What a toss-up!

I don't know about you, but I'd rather face the decisions I typically have to make in a day's time than the ones they were hashing out. As dire as their situation was, their circumstances actually started to look up when it dawned on them that the only option that didn't guarantee death was to go out to the Arameans' camp and surrender to them. If the enemy didn't kill them, they'd at least be able to eat and stay alive. They had an epiphany that they had absolutely nothing to lose!

I find it amazing how much clarity we can have when we're out of options—because I've been there. Sometimes, when we come to our wit's end, it's the very place God wants to meet us. More times than I can count, this is when God has shown up in my life. And that's exactly what He did for the lepers. After their light-bulb moment, they threw caution to the wind and took a risk. They stood up and got to walking.

While they were walking, God did a miracle. He made the Arameans hear the sound of a great army, and they fled before the lepers arrived. As a result, the lepers not only walked into the camp and helped themselves to dinner, but they took for themselves silver and gold and clothing. And then they went back to tell others and their endurance paid off.[13]

By doing something, these men were saved. By doing nothing, they would have died. Running out of options was the best thing that had ever happened to them. Have you ever been there? Are you there now? Are you out of options? At wit's end? It might be the best thing that's happened. Stand up and start walking. Closer to Jesus. Closer to all He has for you. Closer to who He created you to be. Closer to all the purpose He's put in your heart.

Heavenly Father, help me get up and start walking closer to You. Help me do what I can do while You do what only You can do. In Jesus' name, amen.

10 HE WASTES NOT ONE STEP

A person's steps are established by the LORD, and he takes pleasure in his way.
PSALM 37:23

I t wasn't the most glamorous night of my life as a traveling evangelist. I was in my early twenties, sleeping on a cot, doing my best not to wake the three small children under the age of five with whom I was sharing a room. I had been trying to sleep facedown and breathe into my pillow so I wouldn't catch the flu that one of the kids was fighting, but I was so uncomfortable. Exhausted from not really being able to sleep—mostly due to fighting slow suffocation—I tried to turn over, but trying to do so quietly on a creaky camping cot required more dexterity and balance than I had anticipated.

On my first try, I had started to roll over, but the cot and all the covers weighing me down wanted to roll over with me. My next attempt involved gently sliding the covers onto the floor and trying my first move again. Not exactly brilliant, but it seemed worth a shot. Collapsing on my stomach in defeat, I was tempted to laugh, but instead I started to cry. None of this is what I had expected. But it was exactly what I had wanted.

Have you ever felt that way? You prayed and prayed and got what you wanted, but it wasn't what you expected? It's such a strange place to find ourselves in, isn't it?

From the time I was twenty-one, I felt desperate to serve God, and I had prayed fervently for Him to use me. So, every time God gave me an opportunity, I said yes. That's how I found myself crisscrossing Australia for seven years—ministering to youth in country towns. The night I found myself on that cot, I had walked out every yes and faithfully served God, stepping through every open door, even when that meant couch surfing in people's homes. In my walk with God, I had just put one foot in front of the other and trusted Him to direct my steps. Still, no one had told me what a lonely road it can be to build something new, reach for a goal, pursue a dream, and do what you believe God has called you to do. What I didn't understand then was that God was orchestrating my present for my future. He knew what I would do someday, and He was preparing me for the thing He'd prepared for me.

I've come a long way since that night on the cot, but I got from where I was then to where I am now the same way we all do—by taking steps. It's not that one thing led directly to the next thing; it's that one step led to the next step. It was like climbing a set of stairs, and I couldn't bypass any of the steps. What I learned on each step gave me the wisdom, knowledge, strength, confidence, endurance, and maturity to succeed when I moved up to the next one.

Are you ready to take the next step? Keep walking with Jesus because He directs our steps. And He wastes not one step.

Heavenly Father, please lead me in my walk with You, directing my every step. I trust You that not one in my past is wasted. In Jesus' name, amen.

11 IN THE AGE OF SELFIES

Calling the crowd along with his disciples, he said to them, "If anyone wants to follow after me, let him deny himself, take up his cross, and follow me."
MARK 8:34

I am the worst selfie taker on earth. My arms are so short, and I can never get the angle right. Every time I try, my kids beg me to stop. They are mortified at my lack of selfie-taking abilities. One time, when I was hiking up Bishop Pass Trail in the Eastern Sierras, I stopped on a ledge before we reached the summit. Obsessed with getting just the right angle, I almost fell off the ledge. It's definitely best that I leave getting the right shot to someone else, but the pressure to perfect a selfie persists. After all, it's the must-have skill of our generation.

Our obsession with curating a beautiful public profile and placing ourselves in the middle of everything is supposed to lead to greater fulfillment, peace, joy, happiness, and significance, but does it? Sure, we might get a rush when the likes soar, but then we have to get a better selfie to get another rush. And if we don't get the feedback we hope for, we might feel compelled to delete that selfie and post another. All in an effort to get more likes.

Have you ever stopped to think what it would have been like if everyone had been taking selfies with Jesus when He walked the earth? What about when He was saying that if anyone wanted to follow after Him, let him deny himself, take up his cross, and follow Him? Jesus was extending an invitation to die to self in order to find true, abundant life in

Him. I'm not sure there could be a more countercultural message to our generation than this, but the truth is, it would have been as challenging to the followers in Jesus' day as it is to us in the age of selfies.

At a time when we are encouraged to find ourselves, to be self-fulfilled, to protect our self-image, to boost our self-esteem, to be self-confident, Jesus' invitation suggests that if we want to follow Him, then we need to deny ourselves. But denying ourselves doesn't mean we're to minimize or reject ourselves. It means we are to deny our self-trust. Our self-sufficiency. Our self-will. Because, by doing that, we will have the life we actually long for so deeply.

To follow Jesus the way our hearts yearn to, we will have to empty ourselves of something—our self. Then, we will have to put on something—the cross. As much as we might try, we cannot carry both the cross and our self. What's more, in Greek, these three steps Jesus mentioned are in the present continuous tense.[14] Jesus was saying for us to keep on denying ourselves, keep on taking up our cross, keep on following Him. Can you see how it's an ongoing process for a lifetime, to be repeated again and again? Can you see how it builds endurance in us? To deny ourselves, take up our cross, and follow Jesus over and over in our daily lives can't help but build endurance—and endurance is what will keep us following Him. Even in the age of selfies.

Jesus, daily I want to deny myself, take up Your cross, and follow You faithfully. Please help me endure and stay focused on You and the path You've put before me. In Your name, amen.

12 LET'S LOSE IT!

"Whoever wants to save his life will lose it, but whoever loses his life because of me and the gospel will save it. For what does it benefit someone to gain the whole world and yet lose his life? What can anyone give in exchange for his life?"

MARK 8:35–37

I once had the privilege of being with leaders from the underground church in a country where people are not free to worship publicly. I had been asked to come and speak about reaching young people, but when I heard their stories of persecution, suffering, opposition, and faith, I felt so inadequate. In the presence of such faithful Christians, I wasn't sure I really knew what it meant to be a true disciple of Jesus. I remember them explaining to me they had no leadership training beyond being taught how to witness to their prison guard on the way to their execution. I was literally speechless. They knew what it meant to possibly lose their life for the sake of the gospel. I was the one who had much to learn.

Though you and I may not face the prospect of literal death for our faith, I can't help but wonder what it might look like for us to be willing to lose our life wherever we live. To die to our flesh, to pick up our cross daily, to follow after Him. To walk with Him. Closely. Intimately. To keep moving forward building endurance with every step. To stay in faith through each and every circumstance. Trusting Him in the face of anything.

It's not easy, but I'm willing. I'm sure you are too. And I suspect the reason why is because we have a hunger for true life. We desire to find and live life to the full extent that we were created to have it. In today's verse, Jesus acknowledged this by giving us the key to actually finding what it is we so earnestly desire.

We find our lives not by trying to take hold of them ourselves, by trusting ourselves, or by taking care of ourselves. We find our lives by trusting in, depending on, and obeying God. By enduring in faith in every circumstance. If we lose our lives by means of giving ourselves away in the cause of Christ, denying ourselves for Him, then we will find the contentment, inner peace, satisfaction, and purpose that we are actually looking for. None of us wants to lose our soul chasing after things that will never satisfy, and yet it's easy to get caught up in that pursuit and forget what Jesus said.

What if we lose our lives today, the way Jesus described? Because of Him and the gospel? Jesus calls us to an all-in life, but we can't be all in if we keep some things out. So, let's deny ourselves and take up our cross. Let's find our lives in Him and Him alone, the only place where we'll find eternal life, the life we truly want.

Jesus, I want to let go of everything that distracts me from living my life in You, for You, and for the sake of the gospel. Help me lose it today so my life may be saved the way You intended. In Your name, amen.

13 MAKE GOD BIGGER

To him who is able to do above and beyond all that we ask or think according to the power that works in us—to him be glory in the church and in Christ Jesus to all generations, forever and ever. Amen.

EPHESIANS 3:20-21

When my daughter Catherine was little, she used to constantly sing the song, "The mountains are His, the valleys are His, and the stars are His handiwork too. My God is so big, so strong and so mighty, there's nothing my God cannot do."[15]

Like any parent, by the time she'd sung it twenty times a day for twenty days, my ears hurt from the sound of it. In my head it had gone from a wonderful song to white noise. One day, as I was about to tell her to please sing another song, that Mummy couldn't take one more verse, I caught myself. *What am I doing?* I thought. *That is exactly what I want her to know and believe about God. I want her to know that her God is so big and so strong and so mighty and that there is literally nothing her God cannot do. Why would I stop her? She's singing the truth!*

Catherine's singing stopped agitating me and pierced my heart with God's truth. After weeks of hearing her, I finally heard her—and the Holy Spirit. Our God is so big and so strong. He is omniscient, omnipotent, and omnipresent. There's nothing He cannot do. Have you ever heard something so many times that you finally really heard it? And then it felt like you were hearing it for the first time?

Paul said that our God is able to do exceedingly abundantly above all we can ask or think according to the power that works in us. In other words, God can do more than we hope for, contemplate, or consider, but it is according to the faith, confidence, determination, big thinking, and expectation in us. No doubt, God is as big as He will ever be or needs to be. We cannot make Him any bigger than He is, and we don't need to, but the God of the universe is made big or small in the hearts of His people, in your heart and mine.

Do you want God to do something big in your life? Do you see Him as able to do abundantly above all you can ask or think? If we're to keep building endurance, walking into all the purpose and plans God has for our future, then we need to make Him bigger—bigger than our past, than our mistakes, than our disappointments, than our limitations, than our perceptions. We need to make Him bigger than all our fears, all our concerns, and all our reasoning. We need to make Him bigger than anything holding us back.

When we make Him bigger in our hearts and minds, we make that power working in us greater. Greater than what? Greater than whatever it is holding us back from whatever it is God wants us to be and do.

God, please help me make You bigger than all my fears, concerns, anxieties, and everything else holding me back. I want to keep moving forward with You and in You. In Jesus' name, amen.

14 TWO THINGS THAT ENDURE

"You are the salt of the earth. . . . You are the light of the world."
MATTHEW 5:13–14

G rowing up Greek, it wasn't enough that we liberally salted food when we were cooking it; we added even more when we ate it. To sit down to the table and reach for the saltshaker, even before taking a bite, was normal. I've had to learn better eating habits as an adult, but what is it about salty food that makes us so happy?

It can be hard to eat a tasteless steak or a bland piece of chicken, even when we know it's better for our bodies. And don't get me started on the chips and salsa. Chips without salt never feels right. To any food, adding even a little salt can make a huge difference. Sure, we can try all the alternatives, but don't we really want to keep reaching for the salt? I know I do!

Jesus called us the salt of the earth. Why would He do that? Why would He compare us to a seasoning we put on our food? And then He called us the light of the world. Why would He call us the light of the world? Why, of all the things He could have compared us to, did He call us salt and light?

Maybe it's because salt and light are both agents of change. They are catalysts, meaning that by their very makeup, they can't help but change what they come in contact with; yet they don't change. They just effect change, cause change, and initiate change.

When Matthew recorded Jesus' words, there was no refrigeration as we know it, so salt was used to preserve food. It's a method that works so well, we preserve food in the same way to this very day: fish such as cod or herring, meat such as bacon, and vegetables like cabbage and cucumbers. As a catalyst, when we add salt to food, it seasons it or preserves it, but the salt never changes in composition. Salt endures. It doesn't change; it changes things.

When it comes to light, we need only to think about what light does to the dark: It dispels it. It illuminates it. It changes the environment so that we can go from being blind to being able to see. Isn't that why we flip on a light as we enter a room? We don't want to stumble over the coffee table or a pair of shoes that someone kicked off. We want the darkness to be eradicated so we can see. Jesus calls us the light because He calls us into the darkness so our light will overcome it. Light endures. It doesn't change; it changes things.

Salt and light. Agents of change. That's something Jesus named us as part of our identity as His disciples. Something He empowered us to be on the earth and in the lives of other people. Something He wants us walking in everywhere we go.

What's on your agenda today? Remember, as you accomplish all that's before you, keep enduring in faith, being the salt and light Jesus has called you to be.

Jesus, You called me to be salt and light. Help me walk in all that You called and created me to be. Help me be the salt and light You envisioned everywhere I go. In Your name, amen.

15 WALK IN LOVE

This is love: that we walk according to his commands. This is the command as you have heard it from the beginning: that you walk in love.

2 JOHN 1:6

When my mum was in the later years of her life, like many older people, her health began to decline and her memory to fail. It was sad for my brothers and me, especially when we began to see our roles reverse more and more. In the last two years of her life, her need for assistance intensified. She fell several times, often unable to get up on her own, and she was hospitalized more than once. Still, she was insistent that she could manage just fine on her own. She just needed a little help getting up, she'd say.

Though my brothers and I offered, though we talked with her at opportune times, she did not want a full-time caregiver at home, nor was she willing to move to a safer place that offered twenty-four-hour care. When we discussed other options, like one of us and our families moving in with her or her moving in with one of our families, she wouldn't hear it. She wanted to maintain her independence at all costs even though it was becoming increasingly unsafe. For my brothers and me, it was agonizing and, at times, beyond frustrating because no matter what we said, Mum refused to see and acknowledge what was before us.

So many times, I wanted to throw my hands up in the air in frustration and get back on a plane to America where I could be far from my mum's suffering—because, let's be honest, sometimes it feels easier to be compassionate with people who are far away from us than it does with the ones who are up close.

How essential it is, then, that we come before Jesus daily and ask Him to keep the eyes of our hearts open so we can see those closest to us in the same way He does. When we feel rejected or taken for granted by our husbands, children, friends, or colleagues, we can easily default into a defensive posture and harden our hearts—just so we are not hurt. But if we allow our hearts to harden, we will lose the ability to show the love and compassion of Jesus—and therefore lack a vital component of what we require to truly see others as Jesus does.

When my conversations with Mum grew difficult and she would get upset, she wasn't trying to hurt me. She was simply frightened. When I just loved her and quit feeling discouraged or frustrated with her, we got to spend our time enjoying so many laughs and sharing so many good memories.

Maybe you've cared for an elderly parent and can relate. Or maybe there's someone in your life right now whom you find difficult for one reason or another. Sometimes it helps to pause and consider things from their perspective. To acknowledge how they might be feeling. To keep walking in love. Enduring in faith. For Mum and me, it made all the difference.

Father, please help me love the way You love, and to love those around me whom I find difficult to love. I want to walk with You and show Your love to others as I do. In Jesus' name, amen.

16 PRESENT IN THE MOMENTS

Everything exposed by the light is made visible, for what makes everything visible is light. Therefore it is said: Get up, sleeper, and rise up from the dead, and Christ will shine on you. Pay careful attention, then, to how you walk—not as unwise people but as wise—making the most of the time, because the days are evil.

EPHESIANS 5:13–16

W hen my girls were both in their teens, they slept a lot—especially when it was summertime. By the time they got up, I would have had coffee, gone out for a run, dropped by the office, run errands, and eaten lunch. Yes, that means it was usually afternoon by the time they began to stir. Even when our family dog, Ezra Blake, who still sleeps on Sophia's bed, would snore so loud that it sounded like a freight train coming through the walls, both girls slept right through it. I guess to them it must have sounded like a lullaby.

But when it was a school day, well, that was a different story. Both girls had to set their alarms and get up on time. Of course, Nick and I served as the backup system. We'd stop by their doors, listen to hear if there were sounds of life, and take any steps necessary to ensure they were getting ready because if they were not, we all would have been late.

When we would listen at their bedroom doors, sometimes we'd hear nothing. Not a peep. And that's when we'd crack the door, move toward the bed, and shake them awake. If you have had teens, or do now, then you most likely know exactly what I'm talking about. They can sleep like rocks, can't they?

When I read today's scripture and think of how hard my girls could sleep, I can't help but wonder if God sees us the same way sometimes. As people who are sleeping so soundly that we're missing what's happening around us. It occurs to me that it's possible to go through life asleep, fully functioning but not fully awake. That's called sleepwalking, isn't it? I can't imagine that God wants us sleepwalking through life. Because if we do, then we will miss everyone and everything He wants us to see. We'll miss out on all the opportunities He puts before us to effect change, build endurance, and make a difference on this earth. Could it be that by cautioning us to "Get up, sleeper, and rise up from the dead," God is getting us to move from a place of being blurry-eyed to rubbing all the sleepy out to fully opening our eyes so we can see the world around us the way He does? So we can respond to people and circumstances the way He wants us to? So the life and light of Christ will shine on us and through us?

I think so. Did you notice how Paul went on to say that we're to pay careful attention to how we walk, not as unwise people but as wise, making the most of the time? If we're to pay careful attention, we will have to live awake. Alert. Aware of God. Aware of others. Let's do our best to live fully conscious, walking present in the moments He gives us.

Heavenly Father, thank You for all the moments You have given me. Help me be conscious of them and how I'm to use them, so I make the most of them. In Jesus' name, amen.

17 WE ARE ALL THE SPECIAL PEOPLE

You are a chosen race, a royal priesthood, a holy nation, a people for his possession, so that you may proclaim the praises of the one who called you out of darkness into his marvelous light.

1 PETER 2:9

In our home, when I was growing up, Mum never let us use the good crystal glasses she and Dad had received as wedding presents, because we were saving them for when special people came to visit. That was the understanding. I lived at home until I married at thirty, and we never used those crystal glasses. From my vantage point, I guess the special people never came. I've never forgotten this, so I've made it a point in our family to use everything we have. For any kind of occasion.

I tell my daughters, "We are the special people! Get it all out. Set the table with the best crystal and silverware. And if a glass breaks, we'll go buy some more, like some fabulous plastic ones that aren't breakable. Problem solved."

I don't want my daughters to think guests are more worthy or special than they are. Or that a glass is more valuable than they are. After all, we are all chosen, aren't we? Isn't that what Peter was writing? Isn't that the understanding we're to walk in?

What I want my daughters to grow up understanding is that we're "the special people God chose," and at the same time, we're to see everyone else as special too. It's more about how we're to walk with Jesus. When our focus becomes imbalanced—like when we don't necessarily neglect ourselves but do the opposite and zoom in on ourselves too much—it's easy to lose focus of others. Even when people mean well and think they are merely trying to improve their own physical and mental health, they can become too focused on themselves. I understand that we live in a world that is self-absorbed, and as Christ-followers, we strive to never be that way. But what if, in our efforts to endure in faith and to not be self-focused, we simply forget ourselves? Overlook ourselves? Even ignore ourselves? That's not to be our objective either. Nowhere in the Word does it say we're to forget about ourselves. It does say we're to deny ourselves, but denying ourselves is denying our flesh, not our well-being. One builds endurance, and the other doesn't.

Let's find that balance God wants for us. Let's walk with Him, seeing ourselves as He does—as chosen, as a royal priesthood, a holy nation, a people for His possession, designed to proclaim His praises. As people called out of darkness into His marvelous light. As people He loves this much. And let's remember to see everyone else as the same. After all, we are all the special people!

Heavenly Father, I'm so grateful that You chose me. That You called me out of darkness into Your marvelous light. That You made me one of Your special ones. Please help me remember and see others in the same way. In Jesus' name, amen.

18 THE MOST MEMORABLE SCENT

Thanks be to God, who always leads us in Christ's triumphal procession and through us spreads the aroma of the knowledge of him in every place.
2 CORINTHIANS 2:14

I have an obsession with smells. Whether it's candles with scents of vanilla or sandalwood or a waft of freshly ground coffee, a beautiful aroma can make me instantly happy. On the other hand, if I walk into a room in our home and the smell is dull—or repugnant, with volleyball practice shorts and dirty sneakers—I feel compelled to grab a can of air freshener and go running through the house. The onslaught of teenage girl sweat mixed with Sweet Cinnamon Pumpkin can, and actually has, taken my breath away. Why do teenage girls think body spray will hide horrific body odor? I have no idea, but I have learned to buy air freshener in bulk.

Despite how over the top some smells can be—especially the ones at my house—I find the power of how scents can affect us to be fascinating. Smells can evoke such strong emotions in us. When we want to feel better, we can just light a scented candle, and it changes the entire atmosphere around us. Smells have the power to jog our memories and in mere seconds take us back to a time or to a familiar place in our lives. They can even trip flashbacks that throw us into the arms of loved ones gone long ago. To this day, if I walk past a perfume counter, I cannot resist aromatizing myself in Chanel Nº 5. My mother wore it all my life. She always smelled divine to me, and in my memories, my mum was Chanel Nº 5, and Chanel Nº 5 was my mum. There's just no separating the two. Just by spritzing myself, I can smell her walking in the front door with a load of groceries in her arms, and if I let the memory of her smell linger a bit longer, I can begin to see the sparkle in her eyes and hear the joy in her laugh. My dad, on the other hand, was a different story. As elegantly as Mum could pull off the house of Chanel with a trip to the supermarket, Dad was far more basic. He was an Old Spice man, steady and dependable.

When you walk into a room, what do people smell on you? Do you smell like the fragrance of Christ? Are you spreading the aroma of the knowledge of Him everywhere you go? I know we want to, but what if our sweet-smelling fragrance has grown dull or turned sour without our knowing it? It can happen all too easily to any of us. We get busy. We quit enduring in faith. We work up a sweat. We get offended or wounded, and suddenly our fragrance that once wafted a bright floral or a perky citrus scent smells more like dirty sneakers.

Let's freshen up today. Let's be sure we're giving off the sweet-smelling aroma of Christ with our words, our actions, our deeds, and even our smiles. Let's walk into a room and leave the most memorable scent ever.

Jesus, please help me smell like You everywhere I go. Let me walk into rooms and places and hearts and leave Your sweet-smelling fragrance. In Your name I pray, amen.

19 WALKING WITH A SWEET SMELL

To some we are an aroma of death leading to death, but to others, an aroma of life leading to life. Who is adequate for these things?
2 CORINTHIANS 2:16

F lying as much as I do, I've learned to tolerate all kinds of aromas—the tuna sandwich someone brought along, the baby's diaper that needs changing, the fellow who drank coffee before boarding. For him, I have great grace. I only wish that he'd brought me a cup. But there's one smell that I've never adjusted to: the smell of people's feet on a fourteen-hour flight to Sydney from Los Angeles, when they slip off their shoes and stretch out for a nap. Despite my sincere desire to be understanding and think the best of others, I always find it to be one of those moments when I have no words—though I feel sure, given the opportunity without the threat of being restrained by an air marshal, I could think of some.

Watch yourself, now. Don't judge. You know that if you found yourself in the same set of circumstances, you might want to enlighten a fellow passenger as well. We all know that self-awareness is powerful, and when we're lacking it, we need a sister to help us out, right?

In all seriousness, sometimes I think we all need to take a scratch-and-sniff test every now and then. You remember those cute little scratch-and-sniff books, don't you? We had several when my girls were small. I remember how they couldn't wait for me to finish reading each page so they could scratch and sniff the smelly spot. I remember how, if it was a book about fruits, they would scratch on the picture of the purple grapes and sniff that sweet, grapey scent. Even after the books were totally worn out and all I could smell was an occasional whiff of cardboard, they still scratched and sniffed as though we had just bought the book.

In the same way, I think we need to rub shoulders with a trusted friend and ask them how we smell! What if we don't really smell as sweet as we think we do? What if all our scent has worn off? What if the way we actually smell to our families, our coworkers, even complete strangers is completely different from what we perceive? What if we don't smell as gracious or kind or forgiving or patient as we think we do?

You mean people can smell all that? In a sense, yes. How many times have we gone through the checkout line at the grocery store and spoken nice words but our smell reeked of agitation, frustration, and impatience? It's so easy to do, especially when we're distracted by where we need to go next and time is running short.

Changing our smell to be sure we smell as good as we sound or look is one more way we build endurance. Changing our smell to be the aroma of life leading to life, as Paul wrote, is one more way we walk with Christ the way He planned. Sweet-smelling. Fragrant. Like someone everyone wants to be near.

Father, please help me smell like the aroma of life that leads to life. To be sweet-smelling and fragrant to everyone around me. Help me draw people to You. In Jesus' name, amen.

20 WALK THE WALK

Neither the one who plants nor the one who waters is anything, but only God who gives the growth. Now he who plants and he who waters are one, and each will receive his own reward according to his own labor.

1 CORINTHIANS 3:7–8

When Nick and I started following Christ, long before we met, our families didn't know how to process our decisions. We had both been raised in churches with centuries-old traditions, and now we were serving in a very different kind of church. To say it was culture shock to our families doesn't begin to describe it. And when we married, their disapproval didn't stop. We've both sat at many a holiday dinner feeling the concern of our relatives who thought we were going to witness to them by preaching to them. But we never did. We just loved them. For who they were. Right where they were. We did our best to be witnesses of the love and goodness of God every chance we got.

Twenty-five years later—after twenty-five years of holiday dinners—most of our relatives have reached out to us for prayer, for answers to their questions, and for a more meaningful relationship with God. They've invited us in to share with them about our faith and why it's so important to us. Why it makes such a difference in our lives. In our marriage. In our girls. In our passions. In our pursuits. All because we chose to love first and talk second. All because we lived our faith in front of them when they weren't interested in hearing what we might have to say. They've seen us endure in faith over and over.

To be honest, I'm never happier than when I get to testify of Jesus, and yet I equally understand the power of being a witness, a person who walks the walk and doesn't just talk the talk, as we say, especially in a generation that is more lost than found, that's more secular than Christian. Being a witness is something God has called us to be. It's a life that He's called us to live. At times we'll have the opportunity to give voice to that calling, and at times we will simply and quietly love people.

Who are you trying to reach? Is there a person you've been praying for, perhaps for a long time? I imagine we all have someone like that in our lives. It encourages me to understand what Paul wrote: one person plants, another waters, and God gives the increase. This tells me that my part is simply to do what God shows me. To love them, walk the walk in front of them, and perhaps talk only when they ask questions, all the time trusting God to give the increase. To bring them into His kingdom. I've come to understand that nothing can stop me from being a witness, but it is important that I be the right kind of witness at the right time.

The next time you encounter that person you've been praying for, just be content to walk the walk. Plant and water as God directs you. Then trust Him with the increase.

Jesus, please help me be a witness for You in front of everyone I encounter. In my words and my deeds, help me walk the walk everywhere I go. In Your name, amen.

21 AS SURE AS SEEDTIME AND HARVEST

"As long as the earth endures, seedtime and harvest, cold and heat, summer and winter, and day and night will not cease."

GENESIS 8:22

D o you have a dream? An idea? A yearning to do something that just won't go away that you know God has placed in your heart? When God gives us a dream, He is calling forth what He placed inside of us before we were even born. We're full of potential for His plans and purpose for our lives. Still, it's up to us to water the seed of that potential, to tend to the soil of our hearts, to develop all that God has placed inside of us.

Think of it this way: God gave trees the ability to reproduce themselves through their seed. If you've ever taken a pine cone apart, you'll see little seeds, each with a "wing" attached to it. That's so the wind can catch the seed and take it where it can fall to the ground and begin to take root. In the right soil, in the right environment, that seed will sprout and grow into a new, fully grown tree. The fully grown tree was always in the seed, but no one could see it until it was put in the right soil and then nurtured by the rain and the sun.

In a similar fashion, the seeds in our hearts—the dreams and ideas and plans and purposes of God—grow as we water them with faith. The seeds grow as we tend to the soil of our hearts, feeding them the Word of God and applying it in our lives, thus making our hearts good ground. God's plans and purposes for our lives grow as we keep walking with Him, building endurance, and staying with those plans to completion. This is how we give birth to our dreams, to the ideas God gives us. The potential is always there, but it's in seed form until we do what is necessary to make it grow.

God wants us to grow to where we are to go. The challenge is that it's countercultural. It's so much easier to reach for what's instant, for what we can snap and upload, for what we can order and have delivered the same day, but that's not how God's ways work. They aren't instant. God works over time. With a seed that needs to be nurtured.

Are you aware of God's plans for your life? Can you feel any untapped potential lying dormant inside you? Potential is the difference between what is actual and what is possible. It is the unexposed ability, the reserved strength, the unrealized success, the dormant gifts, and the hidden talents waiting to be developed. It is the person you are still to become. It is where you can go but have not yet been. It is all you can do but have not yet done. It is where you can reach but have not yet aimed.

You don't have to know all the plans and purposes God has for you, since most of them unfold over time, but do you know one of them? Start nurturing that seed today and watch it begin to grow. It's as sure as seedtime and harvest.

Heavenly Father, please help me nurture the seeds of potential You have placed inside of me. I want to grow where You want me to go. In Jesus' name, amen.

22 WALK WITH THE WISE

The one who walks with the wise will become wise, but a companion of fools will suffer harm.
PROVERBS 13:20

When I was pregnant with Catherine, I gave up caffeine. Shocking, I know. Up to that point in my life, other than the pregnancy itself, giving up caffeine felt like the greatest miracle I had ever experienced. I was a first-time mum and so eager to create the perfect environment for my baby to grow and thrive. I paid attention to every bite I put in my mouth and mostly drank only water. I was strict about where I went, what I did, and how much I slept. There were no crazy, risk-taking adventures for me, at least not in that season. I'm not sure I was equally strict the next go-round, since I had gained more confidence about what I should and shouldn't do during a pregnancy, but I still cared deeply and watched over everything I ate and what I did. I knew that I was nurturing a child, and what I did had a profound impact on her development.

Since then, as I've come to understand the spiritual significance of giving birth, I see parallels. When we're giving birth to something like a dream or business plan or some other assignment God has placed in our hearts, we monitor every aspect of it so we can cultivate the most positive environment for growth. If we want to see the plans and purposes of God realized in our walk with Him, we can't just do what we want, can we? It's so much like being pregnant physically. There's more at stake than just our craving for coffee.

It matters where we go, what we feed our dream, even who we share it with. If you've ever shared an idea with someone who didn't value it, you know how disappointing that can be. A wise mentor once said to me, "Chris, show me your friends, and I will show you your future." The understanding was that we need to build relationships with those people who are going in the same direction we are and who share the same values. Yes, God often brings people into our lives who are different to stretch us—to expand our horizons, if you will. And He brings people into our lives for us to share the gospel with and to help them become followers of Christ. But when it comes to the plans and purposes of God for our lives, we need to nurture what's growing inside of us the same way we would a baby. We need to feed ourselves spiritually. We need to pay attention to where we go and what we do. And we need to walk with people who are wise, who will encourage us, and who will help us. We need to build healthy, diverse, and challenging relationships that will help us build endurance and reach our dreams.

Are you spiritually giving birth to something? Consider who you're walking alongside. If you walk with the wise, Solomon wrote, you will become wise. And you will deliver.

Father, please teach me how to nurture what You've placed in my heart. Help me surround myself with friends who are wise and who will help me reach my future. In Jesus' name, amen.

23 JESUS ALL OVER YOU

Walk in love, as Christ also loved us and gave himself for us, a sacrificial and fragrant offering to God.

EPHESIANS 5:2

After my mum passed away and my brothers and I met at her house to begin sorting through her things, I couldn't help but pick up a blouse she had worn and just breathe. I understood she was gone, but in that moment, in my heart, she was still there, all because of her natural scent.

We all have a scent like that—an "odortype" some scientific sources call it.[16] It's something we're destined to have and can never escape. It's part of who we are, regardless of what we do or where we go. Unlike our perfumes that we can switch—maybe from a light floral or citrus scent in the daytime to a heavier, more lingering one at night—our natural scent is something we can never change.

But there is a spiritual scent we carry, the fragrance of Christ, and it is something we can change. By becoming fully devoted followers of Christ and spending time with Him, we can go from carrying the smell of our fleshly nature to carrying the sweet-smelling fragrance of Jesus. And the more time we spend with Him, the more we will naturally smell like the fruit of the Spirit, the more we will smell like the character and nature of God. The more we will walk in love. The more we will be found loving, joyful, peaceful, patient, kind, good, faithful, gentle, and given to self-control—something people can figuratively smell on us.[17]

Not sure what I mean? Think of it this way. Have you ever heard someone say, "You could smell the fear all over him"? They mean that figuratively, don't they? Any of us can either smell like a fragrant offering or carry a stench. If we smell like judgment, anger, pride, or condemnation, then people are often repelled by us, aren't they? But if we smell like love, grace, mercy, compassion, and kindness, people want to be around us more. They are attracted to the aroma of Christ, to the way we smell.

Let's spend more time with Jesus so our personal scent—our odortype—becomes just like the fragrance of Christ. I want to smell sweet. When I walk through people's lives, I want to walk in love and waft kindness their way. I want to give off an air of unending patience. I feel sure you do too. Think of the people in your life who need such fruit from you. Make it a point today to endure in faith and show them extra kindness. Extra gentleness. And more love than usual. When you walk through the room, let them smell Jesus all over you.

Father, please continue transforming me from the inside out so I smell like the fragrance of Jesus. Help me walk in love and smell like all the fruit of the Spirit. In Jesus' name, amen.

24 IMITATE GOD

Be imitators of God, as dearly loved children.

EPHESIANS 5:1

Sometimes I think we read verses like this one and wonder, *How do we do what the Word says? How on earth do we imitate God? How could anyone imitate God? After all, He's God. And we're not.* The gap between what we read and figuring out how to live it can feel so daunting, so impossible. And yet I have found that if we're willing to live it, God will be faithful to show us in our everyday walking with Him.

He's done this for me on so many occasions. I remember one summer when Nick and I and our girls were on our way to Norway for me to speak at a youth conference, one of our flights was delayed. That meant making our connection in Frankfurt would be very tight, and we would have to run as fast as we could. While we were waiting to deplane, I noticed an obviously distraught older couple trying to make sense of their boarding passes and connecting flight. They did not seem to speak English or be familiar with the huge airport in Frankfurt and how to get from one terminal to the next.

Watching them, I couldn't help but think of my mother and about how frightened she would be in the same situation. I could see their boarding passes, and their connecting flight was leaving from a different terminal than ours. When we finally got inside the terminal, despite the message boards everywhere, they were still totally lost and frightened. I scanned the gate for assistance, but there were no available agents. I knew

I had to help them. Turning to Nick, who had been watching them too, I told him that if I didn't get back in time to go on without me and I would catch the next flight. It was a risk, but I had endured in faith enough to know it was God nudging me to do something.

I went up to them, immediately challenged by the language barrier, but won their trust. I looked at their tickets, figured out their gate, and motioned for them to follow me. We had a long way to walk, and they didn't have much time, so I maneuvered them through the crowds as quickly as possible. As we arrived at their gate, I motioned to them where to fall in line, but not before the woman turned to me with tears of gratitude streaming down her face. Cupping my face in her hands, she kissed me on both cheeks. Smiling back, I responded with, "Jesus loves you." I wouldn't have missed that moment for the world—and I didn't miss my flight either.

When Jesus walked on this earth, He was willing to be frequently interrupted and inconvenienced. He was often on His way to one place when someone needed help, and He took a detour to meet their need. At times we must be prepared to step aside from our own plan to truly walk in God's purpose. Miracles are waiting in the interruption.

Jesus, please help me imitate You and to walk in love the way You did. Show me whom to help, how to help them, and when to help them the way You would. In Your name, amen.

25 CHALK IT UP TO BINGO NIGHT

I, the prisoner in the Lord, urge you to walk worthy of the calling you have received, with all humility and gentleness, with patience, bearing with one another in love, making every effort to keep the unity of the Spirit through the bond of peace.

EPHESIANS 4:1–3

When my mum was still alive, and after we moved to the US, I would call her almost every week. During each phone call she would lament that she didn't see me enough. So when I planned a trip home to Australia, which I did several times a year, she was always so excited I was coming. And I couldn't wait to see her too. But if I wanted to visit on a Wednesday, she would tell me I couldn't come. Even though I'd call weeks in advance to let her know, and even though I'd reminded her over and over as the date approached, and even though I called her as soon as we landed in Sydney, she was always quick to let me know that Wednesdays were out of the question.

Wednesday night was bingo night, and it didn't matter that I'd flown fourteen hours to see her. Bingo night was bingo night, not family night. Nick and I always laughed about it, but it was still hard to understand. You would think she would move heaven and earth to see me, and she would—just not on bingo night!

To this day when I think of her and bingo night, all I can do is laugh. Yes, sometimes it was frustrating. Sometimes it was exasperating. Sometimes she and all her ways had the power to completely unravel me, but isn't that how family can be? Why is it that the relationships we cherish most can be the ones that try our patience the most? Maybe the answer is simply that. We cherish them and we want those relationships to be the ones that flourish the most. I know that's how I feel about Nick and our girls, about my brothers and their families. I want us to be close. Always.

Paul urged us to walk worthy of the calling we have with humility and gentleness. With patience. Bearing with one another in love. Making every effort to keep the unity of the Spirit through the bond of peace. Even on bingo night. No, he didn't say that last part, but he might as well have. It's easy to walk in all the ways Paul said when no one is challenging us with their version of bingo night, isn't it? It's when their ways—and we all know our family members and their ways—get in the way of our preferences that it is challenging.

Whatever your family is challenging you with today, chalk it up to bingo night, and walk like Paul said. Bear with them in love. Make every effort to keep the unity of the Spirit through the bond of peace.

Heavenly Father, please help me walk worthy of the calling You've given me, with humility and gentleness and patience, always staying in a place of unity. In Jesus' name, amen.

PART 2

PEACE: HIS PRESENCE
IN OUR MINDS

You can't climb a mountain with downhill thoughts.

ANONYMOUS

26 JUMP ON THE RIGHT TRAIN

Set your minds on things above, not on earthly things.
COLOSSIANS 3:2

W hen I was an undergrad student in Sydney, I caught the train every morning from Seven Hills Station in the western suburbs of Sydney where I lived and rode to Redfern Station in the center of Sydney. One morning I was running late and had a lot on my mind because of an important exam, so when I got to the top of the stairs leading to the platforms, I skipped one habitual step: checking the destination board for delays or platform changes. I heard a train pull up to platform 4, immediately rushed down the stairs, and jumped on board as the doors closed. *Just made it*, I thought as I relaxed into a seat.

As the train pulled out of the station, I immediately saw it was going in the exact opposite direction I needed to go—toward the mountains. I began to panic as the train picked up speed and an announcement came over the loudspeaker telling us to enjoy the ride on the express train to Katoomba, in the beautiful Blue Mountains. I felt sick as I realized that I could not get off this train, I was going to miss my exam, and I had no idea when there would be another train to take me back to where I started.

When the train stopped, I rose, still numb from my mistake. The doors opened, and I stepped onto the platform and moaned aloud, "How did I get here?"

The stationmaster happened to be standing nearby. He looked at me with a grin and said, "Well, love, you got on the wrong train, didn't you?"

It was that simple. I had gotten on the wrong train and ended up at the wrong place. How many times do we do this very same thing with our thoughts? Have you ever started your day expecting it to go one way but ended your day wondering how you got to where you were mentally or emotionally? Maybe you found yourself angry, frustrated, lonely, disillusioned, heartbroken, anxious, defeated, or fearful. When that happens, I sometimes imagine that God wants to say to us, "Well, love, you just got on the wrong train of thought, didn't you?"

I've discovered that if I do not manage where I want my thoughts to take me on a daily basis, I will end up jumping on any train of thought, often ending up where I do not want to be—in a place where I'm not enduring in faith. The good news is I can choose where I want to be because I can choose what I think. As Paul wrote to the Colossians, we have the capacity to set our minds—and there's nothing more powerful than a mind that has been set on things above. We do not need to jump on any train of thought that pulls onto the platform of our minds. We can proactively choose to set our minds on the promises and faithfulness of God. We can change the quality of our lives by changing the quality of our thoughts. After all, our thoughts are like a train; they take us somewhere. Let's hop on the right train today.

Heavenly Father, help me set my mind on things above and not on everything else that has the power to derail me today. Help me remember Your promises. In Jesus' name, amen.

27 SHAME FREE

Both the man and his wife were naked, yet felt no shame.

GENESIS 2:25

Of all the things God could have said that Adam and Eve didn't feel when they were naked in the garden of Eden, He said they felt no shame. He didn't say they felt no fear or anxiety or even cold. He didn't say they felt no pain, suffering, anger, insecurity, doubt, or jealousy. He said they felt no shame. I find that so telling. We were created in the image of God to not feel shame, but because of what happened next in Genesis, we all do!

One chapter later, the serpent came, Adam and Eve ate from the fruit of the tree, they realized they were naked, and they hid from God. Shame does that to us, doesn't it? It causes us to hide from God and from each other. It eats away at the core of who we are and what we were created to be. When we're filled with shame, we think something is wrong with us. I know that's how I felt the first few decades of my life. It was like a recording was constantly playing in my head telling me that I was a mistake. That I wasn't any good. That I was somehow less-than. That I was inadequate and fundamentally flawed.

There is no torment like inner torment, and that's what shame is. As hard as we might try, we really can't outrun ourselves and the shame we feel. Try as we might, we can't medicate enough. We can't achieve enough. We can't do enough. All we can do is bring the shame we feel to

Jesus and surrender it to His healing touch. All we can do is invite Him in to transform us and heal us from the inside out.

When we go to Jesus, He is faithful to cover us. He won't shame us more or disgrace us. Think back to the garden of Eden. When God found Adam and Eve hiding in the garden, He covered them. He made skins for them and clothed them. Yes, He removed them from the garden, but not as punishment. He did it to protect them from living in a state of sin forever, and He worked on His plan for Jesus to come so that we all might have eternal life.

When I read today's verse, it is amazing to me that from the outset of creation, God let us know that the perfect state for humankind was that we would feel no shame. No wonder it's one of the greatest things that most of us struggle with all our lives. The Enemy knows how to stop us from enduring in our life of faith, doesn't he?

Where is your mind camped out today? Are you being affected by shame in some way? In your thoughts? In your actions? Invite Jesus in to heal your mind. To heal your emotions. To free you from the effects of shame. As you do, I believe you will come to know what Adam and Eve knew from the beginning—a time when they felt no shame.

Heavenly Father, please come into my heart and mind with Your healing touch. Transform me to think shame-free thoughts and to live free. In Jesus' name, amen.

28 THINK ON THESE THINGS

Finally brothers and sisters, whatever is true, whatever is honorable,
whatever is just, whatever is pure, whatever is lovely, whatever is
commendable—if there is any moral excellence and if there is anything
praiseworthy—dwell on these things.

PHILIPPIANS 4:8

When I first started renewing my mind, I kept sticky notes of handwritten scriptures on my bathroom mirror to remind me of what I needed foremost in my mind. There were verses that reminded me of who I am and what I have in Christ. Verses that reminded me that I am a new creation, that I am the righteousness of God, that I am more than a conqueror in Christ.[18] To this day, sticky notes are still my best friend. Because it took years to develop all the wrong thoughts, it's taken years to renew my mind to the truth so I can think right thoughts.

I know firsthand that despite our best efforts, we can't undo overnight what took so much time to create—all those occurrences of listening to family, friends, teachers, the media, ourselves—so many voices feeding us negative thoughts. But as I have remained committed to the process of replacing my thoughts with God's thoughts, it has continued to transform me and to keep me on track, fulfilling all the plans and purposes of God for my life.

What has profoundly impacted my life is the truth that it really is possible to learn to think a new way. Have you experienced this? For example, have you ever thought about what you think about? And then tried to change it with the Word of God? With God's truth?

Because I'm still working on it, I start every morning filling my mind with the Word of God. I need to remind myself of what God says about me and every circumstance in my life. When I am armed with the truth of His Word, I am able to endure and contend with the daily onslaught of fear, doubt, insecurity, negativity, and lies that the Enemy hurls at me. I do my best to follow what Paul wrote to the Philippians and purposely think on whatever is true, honorable, just, pure, lovely, and commendable. I try to think on anything praiseworthy. I dwell on these things. In the context of our thinking, to *dwell* means "to keep the attention directed on."[19] I keep my attention directed on God and His truths so the lies of the Enemy are less powerful, less dominant, less intrusive, and not in control of my thinking. I know I've grown when a thought that once rattled me instantly no longer has the power to interrupt my day.

Have you put Paul's instructions into practice? Take some time today to think about what you think about. Then, in the areas where you see a need for change, find key verses to start renewing your mind further. It's the best way to keep yourself dwelling on these things: whatever is true, honorable, just, pure, lovely, commendable, and worthy of praise.

Heavenly Father, help me recognize the thoughts that need replacing with Your truth. Illuminate key verses to me that I can memorize, pray, and speak to renew my mind. In Jesus' name, amen.

29 WE HAVE A
SOUND MIND

God has not given us a spirit of fear, but one of power, love, and sound judgment.

2 TIMOTHY 1:7

When the COVID-19 pandemic first started, I remember going to the store one day and being shocked at the empty shelves. I remember overhearing conversations as I waited in the long line at the checkout. While some people had much to say and others very little, what couldn't be missed was the fear in their voices.

On my drive home, I couldn't help but think about it, and when I did, that same spirit of fear began to invade my mind. I thought of my girls and how all this could affect them. They'd already been sent home from school to learn online. They'd already been separated from their friends and routines. We all were adapting to a whole new way of life minute by minute.

As I pulled into the driveway, deep down, I knew I couldn't go in the house in such a state. I had to stop and rein it all in. For Nick. For the girls. For my own peace of mind. So, doing what I had done a thousand times before, I put my hand to my forehead, and I started talking to myself: "Christine, God has not given you a spirit of fear but of love, power, and a sound mind. You might not understand what is happening, but the one thing you know is that God has never failed you before, and He is not about to start now, so you know you can trust Him now."

I understand you might think this is a strange ritual, but it is a practice I have developed over the years. When I have a decision to make. When I need answers in a tough situation. When my thoughts begin to spiral, my heart starts to race, and my palms go damp. When everything feels out of my control, and fear wants to take complete control. When I need to endure in faith.

In every battle we face, our fiercest enemy is fear—and the devil knows it. That's why he's always ready to foster it and reinforce it. If we don't learn how to overcome its power, then it can defeat us every time. It can even develop into chronic conditions that manifest in our bodies and minds, such as anxiety, panic attacks, incessant worry, or sleepless nights. If you have ever suffered from any of fear's debilitating effects, you know that the symptoms are very real.

But God has not given us a spirit of fear. He has given us power, love, and sound judgment. The Bible translation I first memorized calls it a "sound mind," which is why I quote it that way to myself.[20] I do my best to use God's Word to defeat fear where the battle always begins—in my mind.

What about you? Have you learned to fight the battle in your mind and for your mind? Have you learned to wield God's Word against the fear that tries to take over? Today's verse is a strong declaration to remind yourself that God has not given us a spirit of fear but of power, love, and a sound mind.

Heavenly Father, thank You that You have not given me a spirit of fear but of power, love, and a sound mind. Help me remember this and keep trusting in You more. In Jesus' name, amen.

30 YOU ARE ABSOLUTELY BEAUTIFUL

You are absolutely beautiful, my darling; there is no imperfection in you.
SONG OF SONGS 4:7

When Catherine was in kindergarten, she and a little boy in her class began fighting over a teddy bear. At one point, the little boy ripped the bear from her hands and said, "Catherine Bobbie, you are dumb and ugly!"

What she did next astounds me to this day, and I am so grateful. The teacher told me that she squared her shoulders back and said, "No I'm not. My daddy says that I'm intelligent and beautiful!"

What the teacher had no way of knowing was that's exactly what Nick has said to our girls for as long as I can remember. Every night since they were born, he has prayed with them and told them who they are in Christ. He has reminded them year after year that they are created on purpose and for a purpose, that they are intelligent and beautiful, that they can do whatever God has called them to do, and they can be whomever God has called them to be. He tells them in every way he can what the Word says about them.

Nick knows that our world today tells women, young and old alike, just the opposite. That they are not enough in so many ways—not thin enough, not pretty enough, not talented enough, not smart enough, not young enough, not old enough, and on I could go. I'm so glad that because

Catherine knew the truth of what God says about her, she avoided years of torment—all because she knew who she was. Had some little boy said that to me, because of the trauma I had experienced from abuse, abandonment, and adoption, I would have been paralyzed. I would have had no idea what to do except to let it affect me. Deeply. For years to come.

It was only when I gave my heart fully to Christ, when I began to learn who I was in Christ, that I learned how to deflect the darts of the Enemy. That is when I began letting what Christ did for me become bigger than what others had done to me—or said about me. Knowing who I am in Christ is one of the most powerful ways I endure in faith. I know who I am, in Christ.

Has someone voiced something deeply wounding to you? Has it affected you more than you thought it would? Maybe it's time you sorted out the lies of the Enemy from the truth of who God says you are. Knowing more of who you are in Christ is the best way to overcome the lies that have been told to you. Run to God and His Word today. Read the truth and declare it over your life. You could start with the Song of Songs (also known as the Song of Solomon). It's where God says, "You are absolutely beautiful."

Heavenly Father, help me learn how to tell Your truth from lies I've heard. Help me know Your Word and discover more of who I am in Christ. In Jesus' name, amen.

31 THIS MARATHON CALLED LIFE

Do not be conformed to this age, but be transformed by the renewing of your mind, so that you may discern what is the good, pleasing, and perfect will of God.

ROMANS 12:2

I love to run, though I'm totally not a serious runner. My idea of running is a five-mile slow jog, and when I say slow, I mean mothers pushing their babies in strollers can overtake me. My friend Dawn, the one I hike mountains with, is the real runner. She regularly competes in marathons and has built both the physical and mental endurance to go such distances. She's run enough to know what it's like to hit a wall while running, a concept I've never experienced because apparently I've never run far enough!

Hitting a wall is a place runners can overcome only with their minds. It's more mental than physical, even when the physical is excruciating. Dawn once explained it to me by describing what happened in her first marathon. She was twenty-three miles in when she hit the infamous wall. She had thirty-six minutes to cover the remaining 3.2 miles. It would not have been an issue had she not already run for miles and didn't have searing pain pounding in her left hip. As she tells it, the left side of her brain (the rational side) told her to stop and walk the rest of the way. Thoughts like, *Don't worry about meeting the goal. People will understand when they realize how hot it is and how badly I hurt,* thundered in her head. But just as loud, the right side of her brain thundered back, *There is still hope! The race isn't over yet! It's still possible to meet my goal. Don't stop running!*

Have you ever felt yourself in such a mental war? When your mind is screaming at you? In a race this happens when you hit a wall, when you have nothing left to give, when you've expended every ounce of energy and everything within you wants to quit. And yet, as Dawn experienced, somewhere deep inside, the flicker of a goal or dream begs to not be extinguished.

I've been in such a place, where I hit a wall spiritually, mentally, and emotionally. But at the same time, I had the Word of God in my heart and mind. I had God's promises resounding in me at the same time my mind was screaming for me to stop. And because of His promises, that flicker of hope, I was able to keep going by focusing my mind on God and His Word. Despite how many times my mind fought me to quit, I kept redirecting my mind away from what it wanted to think and toward what God's Word said was true.

Maybe you're in such a place right now. What is your mind screaming at you? That it's not possible? That it's too late? That you're not equipped? Not smart enough? Young enough? Old enough? Educated enough? You can win the war in your mind by renewing it with God's words. You can endure by making God's voice louder than any other voice in your head.

Heavenly Father, thank You for Your Word. Help me be more acquainted with what it says so I can be transformed by the renewing of my mind, and so I can get through any wall. In Jesus' name, amen.

32 JESUS SETS US FREE

"Do not be afraid, for you will not be put to shame; don't be humiliated, for you will not be disgraced. For you will forget the shame of your youth, and you will no longer remember the disgrace of your widowhood."
ISAIAH 54:4

I spent the first twenty-two years of my life looking through a filter of shame. From as far back as I have any memory, I can never remember a time when I did not feel ashamed as a child and for many of my adult years. It was all I knew. I felt it when I was abused and couldn't tell anyone, and believed it was somehow my fault. I felt it when I tried to hide or apologize for who I was, to minimize my talents, or to overachieve and compensate for feeling somehow less-than. I felt it when I was rejected and made to feel unworthy, made to feel of no value.

Have you felt it? If you're human, I would imagine so, and the result is always the same. Shame is the fear of being unworthy, and it adversely affects our relationship with God, ourselves, and others. It greatly hinders our ability to receive God's unconditional love and then to share it with others. I wish I could say that as soon as I decided to follow God and dedicate my life to serving Him through helping others, the shame in my life disappeared. But unfortunately, that's not how shame works.

I expected that once I'd left my old life and joined God's team, I would feel free and could simply forget the past and move on. But I didn't.

I was forgiven and had access to all the promises of God in Christ Jesus, but I still carried a broken heart, a wounded soul, and a tormented mind because shame disrupts those internal settings.

Walking with God to work through and fight against the shame in my life has been my single most difficult journey. But doing the hard work of healing is the only way we can get to the other side, to the place of freedom fulfilling our future. It's more about how we endure in our faith.

Because of God's great love, I began to discover the power of His Word to break through the lies I had believed and to reveal the truth of who I am and why I was created. Notice the key word in that sentence is *began*.

Walking free from shame is not something that happens in an instant. Instead, it's an amazing adventure of enduring, a journey of discovering the depths of God's unconditional love and the broad scope of His power to transform our hearts and minds. Today's verse makes this clear. God created you for a unique purpose. He has a specific plan for your life. And guess what? Shame has no place in that purpose or plan. Jesus came to set you free from shame, so let Him do a work in you!

Jesus, I trust You that I will not be put to shame. Help me move forward and be set free from all the shame that has chased me. Help me fulfill all the plans and purposes You have for my life. In Your name, amen.

33 JESUS SPEAKS ABSOLUTE TRUTH

"You are of your father the devil, and you want to carry out your father's desires. He was a murderer from the beginning and does not stand in the truth, because there is no truth in him. When he tells a lie, he speaks from his own nature, because he is a liar and the father of lies."
JOHN 8:44

When I was elementary-school age, my mother enrolled me in a ballet class. But, being the unconventional girl I was, as soon as she'd wave bye and drive off, I'd drop my tutu to the ground and run across the street to play soccer with the boys. Ballet was boring. Soccer was full of nonstop action. My antics worked well until Mum caught on, and then she told all my aunts, because nothing in our family was ever private. In our family, if one knew, fifty knew. And everyone felt the freedom to speak to you about anything, including skipping ballet.

I remember when one of my aunts spoke her mind. I feel sure she meant well, but what she said affected me deeply. "Christine," she said, "you should prefer ballet to soccer. You're not feminine enough."

Though it was years before I was mature enough to process what she actually said, the message was clear because it included that all-too-familiar word *enough*. I had heard it for years. Not good enough. Not smart enough. And now, not feminine enough. Her words became one more lie of the Enemy that I believed about myself, because, until I turned my life over to God, I didn't know how to defeat such lies. I remember how I even took up repeating such lies to myself and to others. Isn't that what we do when we don't realize the Enemy's work? I can remember saying things like "No one will ever love me," or "I'm a failure," or "I'm damaged goods."

Have you ever said such negative things? I imagine that if we heard one of our daughters or friends saying such things, we'd be so quick to interrupt with affirming words of love and life, wouldn't we? And yet, until we know better, it's so easy to mistakenly join in the Enemy's chorus. Jesus said that Satan is the father of lies and accuser of us all. When he lies, he speaks his native tongue, and when we join in with those lies, it seems all our emotions and feelings follow along. It seems to only reinforce what's not true.

When I began to learn what God says and thinks about me, and when I began to believe it and then say it, my life changed. To realize that I shouldn't believe all my feelings and thoughts, especially when they contradict the Word of God, was a game-changer.

I don't know what lies are tormenting you today, but to keep enduring in faith, you will need to put a stop to them—and you can. Start replacing them with the absolute truth of God's Word. Sure, you'll still hear the Enemy speaking his lies, but you won't ever have to believe them or repeat them again.

Heavenly Father, help me defeat the Enemy's lies with Your words of life and truth. Help me repeat what You say about me, and nothing the Enemy says about me. In Jesus' name, amen.

34 AS WE LOVE
OURSELVES

"Love the Lord your God with all your heart, with all your soul, with all your strength, and with all your mind," and "your neighbor as yourself."
LUKE 10:27

From the time I understood this verse, I endeavored to live it, but like we all discover, some things are easier said than done. I'll never forget when Nick and I were engaged, he told me that he had one goal in life: "I want to love you as much as you do."

I thought I obviously gave off a great deal more confidence than perhaps I should have, or maybe he was just blinded by love, but to be honest, it was neither. The statement Nick made was tongue in cheek; I still had plenty of challenging days that he got to witness firsthand. Back then, I had a *long* way to go in my sanctification process—and I'm still a work in progress today—but if you had known me then, you would know how far I really have come. How much I loved myself at that point was nothing short of a miracle, because I had spent so many years ashamed of myself. The fact that I had gotten to a point where I could let Jesus do a work in me—to the point that I not only liked myself but also was beginning to flourish in life and even love myself—was a testimony to the goodness of God, the power of God, and His unending love for me.

I know firsthand from my journey that when our hearts have been broken, we can feel exposed, vulnerable, weak, insecure, inferior, discontented, or envious. When our souls have been wounded, we can suffer trauma and feel shame, guilt, or condemnation. When our minds have not been renewed, we can believe lies about our identity and self-worth—and experience unbelief, torment, and suffering. Even our upbringing, culture, traditions, education, and exposure to the world can interfere with our loving our neighbor as ourselves. Still, I've never stopped trying to do this well.

Wouldn't it have been great if Jesus had just said for us to love God with all our hearts, souls, strength, and minds, and end it there? It seems that by adding "and your neighbor as yourself," He threw in all the really hard work. Doesn't it feel far more comfortable thinking of Christianity as loving God only? Loving the Lord your God with all your heart, soul, and mind? I certainly think so. But Jesus wasn't giving us a choice of loving God *or* loving people. He was telling us we are to love God *and* people. The challenge is that we are not supposed to love people in the way we love God—we are supposed to love people the way we love ourselves. But, for some reason, loving ourselves seems to be the hardest of all.

Wherever you are on the journey to loving yourself more, keep enduring so you can love others better than ever. Maybe take an extra moment today to care for yourself more. To rest or read a book or do what gives you greater peace. Whatever you do, let it be more of loving God with all your heart, soul, strength, and mind so you can love others as yourself.

Heavenly Father, help me continue to love You with all that I am, and to love myself so I can love my neighbor as myself. In Jesus' name, amen.

35 SIMPLIFY YOUR LIFE

You will keep the mind that is dependent on you in perfect peace, for it is trusting in you.

ISAIAH 26:3

One thing God has allowed me to do over the course of my life is to keep my journey of following Him very simple. I find that the simpler I keep my life in this very complex world—including my spiritual life—the more peace I have. So, every now and then, I find it's good to declutter my heart and my mind. To take an inventory of what I'm carrying around—spiritually, mentally, emotionally, and even physically. To ask myself, *Have I picked up some baggage I need to drop? Have I made it all harder than I need to?*

I find it interesting that we have an entire simplification and minimalization industry in the world today because people are overwhelmed by clutter. Personally, I have found that the more decluttered my home is, the more decluttered my mind is. Nick and my girls will tell you that I am the purge queen. If I buy two new shirts, I give away two old shirts. In our home, there is a place for everything and everything in its place. It's part of how I keep life simple.

In fact, as strange as it may sound, when I started climbing mountains, I had no idea how it would serve to fuel my passion for keeping life simple. I discovered that when I reach a summit, there is a kind of peace like no other that comes over me. I may be gasping for air, desperate to sit down and rest, but despite how exhausted my body may feel, I can't escape seeing what God has made and stand in awe of His overwhelming greatness. My mind can't help but rest on Him. Being that high on the planet, sometimes as high as 11,000 feet, when all I can see is other mountaintops and forests, I feel above the fray of all things human. Not to sound too lofty, but I truly feel closer to the Divine. Who else can make such beauty? Who else can put so much into perspective with one glance? And bring such order and peace? No one but God.

It's in those moments, when I take in the sweeping 360-degree view, I have no doubt there is a peace available to us that is supernatural. It defies understanding. It does not make sense—because it comes from God. Whatever I might have been dealing with at the start of any trailhead—problems to solve, relationships to resolve, issues to sort—when I reach a summit, that situation seems replaced by what matters more: the peace of mind that comes from trusting in and depending on God. And God alone.

Are you short on peace today? Maybe it's time to take an inventory and declutter your heart and mind. Maybe it's time to make things simpler so you can save your strength for your purpose. Do whatever it takes for your mind to rest on God and be dependent on Him, so you can endure, fulfilling all that He's created you to be and all that He's called you to do.

Heavenly Father, help me simplify my life and keep my mind dependent on You, resting on You so I stay in perfect peace. Please show me how I can declutter my mind. In Jesus' name, amen.

36 DID GOD REALLY SAY?

Now the serpent was the most cunning of all the wild animals that the LORD God had made. He said to the woman, "Did God really say, 'You can't eat from any tree in the garden'?"

GENESIS 3:1

At any given time, I always have a few yet-to-be-Christian friends in my life, and I hope they'll come to a place of asking about my faith in Jesus and invite Him in. I never want to get away from being salt and light in a world that desperately needs more or from doing what Jesus commissioned us all to go and do—make disciples. I never want to get away from doing life with the people who need Jesus the most. So, as often as I can, I go and have coffee with one of my friends or catch up with them for a walk. I enjoy that we talk about most everything—politics, marriage, parenting, a favorite new movie, the latest novel, what we bought on sale, or working out. And, naturally, I get excited when the conversation turns to faith.

Those conversations can go in any direction and be about any topic. I have to admit, it's funny when someone quotes something and you know it more likely came from a fortune cookie than it did the Bible. I don't fault my friends, of course, because even as Christians it's all too easy to misquote the Word. Have you ever been guilty of quoting something you thought was in the Bible only to learn later that it wasn't? Perhaps you were repeating something your grandmother always said, but when you read that scripture, you discovered your grandmother didn't have it quite right.

We live in a world where there is so much false information and opinion that it's incredibly easy to think the wrong thing. The only way to be sure we're thinking the right thing is to read and study the Word. If we're not reading it, then it's easier to be misinformed or to be misled by a lie—a lie the Enemy spins to deceive us, if even a little bit. But a little bit can make a huge difference.

Think back to when the serpent spoke to Eve in the garden of Eden. He twisted the truth and challenged God's character. He began by asking the question, "Did God really say . . . ?" Isn't that what he's still doing to us today? The Enemy continues to target us by trying to undermine our confidence in God and His nature by asking, "Did God really say?"

This is dangerous to our enduring in faith because if we don't know what God has said, we will believe the lies of the Enemy however he spreads his tales. We'll believe what we hear at the office. We'll believe what we see on social media. We'll believe anything anyone tells us. It's important that we know what God has said so when the Enemy says, "Did God really say?" instead of adopting wrong beliefs or growing doubtful, we will begin to declare God's truth. We'll know the truthful answer when the Enemy says, "Did God really say?"

Heavenly Father, please help me know and understand Your Word, Your truth. Cause what I read and study to come to mind to help me discern the Enemy's lies. In Jesus' name, amen.

37 RECOGNIZE THE REAL ENEMY

Although we live in the flesh, we do not wage war according to the flesh, since the weapons of our warfare are not of the flesh, but are powerful through God for the demolition of strongholds. We demolish arguments and every proud thing that is raised up against the knowledge of God, and we take every thought captive to obey Christ.

2 CORINTHIANS 10:3–5

From the time I started school, I loved it. I remember as early as second grade being beyond excited to see my report card because I knew I had done well. Once, though I was supposed to carry it home in a sealed envelope to my parents, I opened it before I got there. My heart swelled with a sense of achievement when I saw one high mark after another, but when my eyes landed on what was written at the bottom, it sank just as quickly. "Christine is an excellent student, but she has to learn that she can't always be the leader."

That statement changed what I believed about myself for years. Yes, I liked being the leader. I had been rejected for so many things, but I noticed that when we broke into groups, others followed my lead. If a question stumped my classmates, they turned to me for the answer. But all that vanished when I read the comment. My little second-grade mind internalized: *Don't be seen as bossy. Don't be seen as pushy. The best thing to do is shrink back and hide.* I doubt I thought it so clearly, but by the end of the school year my final report card confirmed that I had interpreted it correctly: "Christine has settled down very nicely."

I probably did need to refine my leadership enthusiasm, but those words quenched the flame God had given me. I let them affect me all the way into my twenties. As an adult, I'd go into work environments and remind myself, *Christine, don't be too full-on or people won't know how to take you. Watch your tone. Don't come across with too much enthusiasm. People don't know what to do with a woman like you.* And, naturally, I started out in a career where I was often the only woman at the table.

It's amazing how cunning the Enemy can be and how quickly he can build a stronghold in our hearts that can take years to demolish—especially in the area of our calling. It's so important that we learn to take every thought captive to obey Christ—so we don't live out any of the lies we've internalized. So we can endure in who He's created us to be and what He's called us to do.

God never wants anything He has put inside of us to be quenched. Is there a lie that has caused you to diminish yourself? To live far beneath your potential? To hide from the plans and purposes God has for your life? Recognize who the real Enemy is at work in your life. Then use God's Word to demolish any strongholds that have been built. Take every thought captive to obey Christ. And dare to be everything God made you to be.

Heavenly Father, please help me see who my real Enemy is in every situation. Help me take every thought captive and think only what aligns with Your Word. In Jesus' name, amen.

38 DROP THE FIG LEAF

He [God] asked, "Who told you that you were naked? Did you eat from the
tree that I commanded you not to eat from?"

GENESIS 3:11

W hen I was growing up, I completely stressed my traditional
Greek mother. "Christine," she often said, "if you keep reading
books, and you get too smart, no man is going to want to marry you." She
meant well, but the way my mother was raised, and the way she wanted
to be sure I was raised, girls were to learn to cook and keep house. Not
read too much or go to college or do anything that might make them
appear smarter than their future husbands. Archaic, I know. But in our
culture, that's how it was.

None of that was the reason I didn't marry until I was thirty. I just
didn't find the man of my dreams until then. But Mum's comments set me
up to feel ashamed—so much that when I got around men, particularly
in a work setting, I dumbed myself down. Knowing who I am today, it's
hard to imagine, but it's true. I would literally work at not letting any man
know all that I knew. My Greek culture was so deeply embedded in the
fabric of my being that I did this automatically and often subconsciously.

Have you ever done anything even remotely close to this? It's tempting
to hide some of ourselves when we get in circles where we fear rejection
for what we're actually good at doing. We may even hide the best part
of ourselves.

In the early years of my career, I often found myself in rooms full of men who were older than me, who had worked years longer than me, and I could tell, for the most part, they weren't going to listen to much of what I had to say. So I did what I had been taught to do: shrink back and hide. Even though I was a woman made in the image of God, created to be what God had planned, called to do what God had purposed, in those settings, it's like I became my own worst enemy. I was just as guilty for holding myself back as any of them might have been, had I given them the opportunity. Regardless of their possible behavior, I was responsible for mine.

It's as though I acted like Adam and Eve did when they hid after eating the fruit. God came looking for them and found them covering their nakedness with fig leaves. He asked, "Who told you . . . ?" Perhaps we need to ask ourselves the same question: "Who told you, Christine, to fear being too smart? Who told you to hide your intelligence? Who told you to not share your ideas, creativity, zeal, enthusiasm, and passion? Who told you? Who?"

God didn't tell Adam and Eve to hide any more than He's ever told us to hide. Hiding isn't from Him, and it will most certainly keep us from enduring. So the next time you're in a circle where you're tempted to hide, drop the fig leaf and be all that God created you to be.

Heavenly Father, help me have the courage to quit hiding, to be seen according to Your divine design. Thank You for creating me in Your image for everyone to see. In Jesus' name, amen.

39 A DOUBLE PORTION
OF JOY

In place of your shame, you will have a double portion; in place of disgrace, they will rejoice over their share. So they will possess double in their land, and eternal joy will be theirs.

ISAIAH 61:7

I find it astounding how crafty the Enemy can be at getting into our heads and influencing so much of what we think about ourselves. What's more, the thoughts that easily consume me can be completely different from the ones that consume you. How does he have the time to be so precise? I have no idea, but what I do know is that each of us has to fight to keep shameful thoughts away and hold on to our peace of mind.

Through the years, as I've worked to keep my peace, I have noticed I have certain triggers. You know, those seemingly innocuous things people might say or do that can send me spiraling in my thoughts. That can make me feel shame in an instant, and sometimes debilitate me, if even for a minute. It's those times I can't wait to get alone and process what was said or what happened and get it into a clearer perspective.

You would think after so many years of following Jesus nothing would have the power to rattle me anymore, especially with all I've overcome, but I think we all have our triggers. They seem woven into our human frailty.

Granted, what might have paralyzed me for days in years past, I am now quick to recognize as the Enemy and his schemes. Still, it's as though the Enemy always knows how to up his game; and there's always something he can use to divert my attention, if even for a short period of time. How important it is then to lean into God and His Word so I stay focused and on mission.

What about you? What are your experiences with the Enemy's craftiness? Can you see how he works in our lives to undermine our joy, our confidence, our hope, our faith, our ability to endure on this earth? He is ruthless, which is why sometimes we have to be ruthless too. Not to people who might say or do something hurtful, but in how we protect our hearts and minds.

I have found that we will always be too much for some people and not enough for others. Some people will like us and some people won't. And some people will inadvertently say things that trigger shame and other negative emotions in our hearts. It just happens. But the good news is that we do not have to stay in the spiral of shame and defeat. We can replace the lies of the Enemy with the truth of the Word of God and walk with our heads held high as sons and daughters of the King.

Father, please show me how to silence the voices that trigger shame in me so I can keep my peace of mind as well as my joy, confidence, hope, and enduring faith. In Jesus' name, amen.

40 RUN TO THE ONE LOOKING FOR YOU

The man and his wife heard the sound of the LORD God walking in the garden at the time of the evening breeze, and they hid from the LORD God among the trees of the garden.

GENESIS 3:8

When my girls were younger, like all kids, if they got caught doing something we had instructed them not to do, their reaction was to cover it up. To not give full disclosure. Dare I say even be a bit vague on explaining what they did and why. As a mother, I never stopped being amused at their creative answers or at how there are some things we don't have to teach our kids to do. Like lie. But then again, we all arrive on the planet innately wired to save our own skin, don't we?

I remember one of the times Sophia tried to cover up after she got caught red-handed. She was probably four or five and begged for ice cream after dinner. I said no because she had enjoyed plenty of treats all week long and it was time to rein it in. But later that evening, long after I'd put her to bed, I came downstairs to find the kitchen illuminated by the open freezer. I couldn't see who was hiding behind the door, but I had a pretty good idea. "Sophia, is that you? Are you into the ice cream?"

"No, Mum," she said, which was the first dead giveaway that all my insanely accurate mother's intuition was spot-on. The second was how she said it. Muffled. Garbled. Because her mouth was full of ice cream!

When she peeked around the corner of the door, the sides of her mouth were covered in chocolate.

It was all I could do not to burst out laughing. I've always had to stay two steps ahead of Sophia because, well, she's a clever girl whose wheels are always turning—no idea where she got that from. But I was never sure what she would do next. So eating ice cream straight out of the bucket with the freezer open was no surprise. And trying to swallow fast and cover up what she was doing—well, that's been going on since time began. Literally.

Is that what's at the heart of today's verse? When Adam and Eve knew sin for the first time, in an instant, they felt what they had never felt: shame. And because of that, when God came looking for them, they hid.

Isn't that how shame affects us to this day? When we make a mistake, doesn't shame make us want to run for cover? It's a good thing that God is faithful. Just like He came looking for Adam and Eve, He always comes looking for us. If you've messed up, there's only one way to keep enduring. Run to the One who is looking for you. He loves you. He is for you.

Heavenly Father, help me remember when I make a mistake not to cover it up. Whether it's something I've done or said, help me run to You, the One who created me to know no shame. In Jesus' name, amen.

41 THERE YOU ARE!

The LORD God called out to the man and said to him, "Where are you?" And he said, "I heard you in the garden, and I was afraid because I was naked, so I hid."

GENESIS 3:9–10

When Sophia was not even a year old, she loved to play a little game. She would cover her eyes and wait for me to ask in a singsong voice, "Sophia, where are you?" And then she would wait in silence. What was so funny about this game is that Sophia thought that because she covered her eyes, I couldn't see her and that I would never find her. But I was sitting there looking right at her. After a suspenseful second, when she couldn't stand it anymore, she would drop her hands and wait for me to respond in utter surprise and delight that I had found her. "There you are!" I'd exclaim. Like any mother, I loved playing our little game, but after a few rounds, I was ready to move on. But not Sophia. She could have stayed with it for hours.

Sophia is long past such baby games, but when I read today's verse, I can't help but think of her and remember how she thought that because she couldn't see me, I couldn't see her. I wonder if that's what Adam thought. When God spoke to both Adam and Eve, "Where are you?" surely God knew exactly where they were; after all, He's God. He's omniscient, which means He is all knowing. All the time. For all time. Including that day in the garden.

Somehow I think there's more to that question. Perhaps it was just

God's way of reaching out to Adam. To connect with him. Maybe He's still asking the same question today of us. Maybe it's His way of reaching out to us. To get us to connect with Him. Because shame and so much more in this world is always at work to disconnect us from Him. Just like it was for Adam.

Do you ever feel Him calling out to you the way He called out to Adam? There are times when I think He calls out to us personally, specifically, intimately: "Where are you? I made you to have fellowship with you. I made you because I love you. I made you in My image. Where have you gone? Where is the you that I created? Where is that personality I gave you? Where are those talents I gave you? Where is the real you?"

Do you realize that God doesn't ask such questions because He doesn't know the answer? He asks because He wants us to find what we have been hiding. Our purpose. Our calling. Our joy. Our peace. Our endurance. Our truest self. He wants us to be freed from the shame and guilt and condemnation that often send us hiding. He wants us to quit hiding in plain sight. He wants us to drop our hands and uncover all that we are so He can exclaim in utter delight, "There you are!"

Heavenly Father, help me not to hide any part of myself any longer. Help me uncover all that You created me to be so I can do all that You called me to do. In Jesus' name, amen.

42 MORE LIKE CHRIST

Who has known the Lord's mind, that he may instruct him? But we have the mind of Christ.

1 CORINTHIANS 2:16

While I have run for most of my adult life, I haven't always had the best form. In fact, there was a time when I had such sharp pains in my right hip, I finally gave in and went to see a physical therapist. True to who I am, I remember saying, "Can we deal with this quickly? I have a half-marathon coming up and I need it to be healed by then." At which he laughed. I truly had no idea how much damage I had done by not stretching before each run and then running with poor form.

When he told me that I wouldn't be running in any race for the rest of that year, I was surprised. I never understood the importance of running the right way. I had always just laced up my shoes and headed out the door. It took time, but I did adjust mentally to a new reality, and I started working on it.

What made all the difference was my being willing to put in the time needed for my hip to recover. I learned new stretching exercises and practiced them. I learned exercises I'd never done before to strengthen the muscles surrounding my hip. And I changed the way I intentionally put my feet down on the pavement. It was a lot of work, but it paid off. After almost a year of therapy, I found the pain subsiding, and my hip eventually healed completely. To this day I still get to enjoy running.

But truth be told, the change had to first take place in my mind. Ever hear the saying, "Half the battle is a made-up mind"? In many circumstances in our lives, it feels so true. To begin learning to do something new we have to first process it with our minds. It certainly was the case for me. Once I got over the shock, processed the changes necessary in my life, and began moving forward with those changes, I eventually saw results in my body.

Isn't this how we move forward spiritually? Don't we have to first wrap our minds around something and then intentionally embrace it? Isn't that how we endure mentally and spiritually? Paul wrote to the Corinthians telling them they had the mind of Christ. Having the mind of Christ is seeing things through His eyes and with His perspective. It's understanding the situations in our lives from His vantage point and from the perspective of the Word.

When was the last time you changed your mind about something? When was the last time you exchanged your thinking for God's thinking? God likes it when we change our minds, when we go from thinking what we've understood to thinking the way He thinks. It's how we continue to be transformed in our minds. It's how we become more like Christ.

Heavenly Father, help me endure more with the mind of Christ. Help me exchange what I think for what You think, for what's in Your Word. I want to see things the way You do. In Jesus' name, amen.

43 TIME FOR A CHANGE

From then on Jesus began to preach, "Repent, because the kingdom of heaven has come near."

MATTHEW 4:17

As strange as it may sound, before I began following Jesus whole-heartedly, I'm not sure I gave any thought to the things I was thinking about. All I knew to do was think whatever popped into my mind, or to think what someone else suggested, or to think what I had always been led to believe was true—whether it was or not. As a young girl I can remember hearing people say things like "God's just angry" or "God can't forgive that," so naturally, I adopted those perspectives. I didn't know not to. I had never heard anyone say anything to the contrary, not that anyone really ever talked about God much. And I didn't really read the Word for myself until I was grown, so there was no reason to challenge what I was hearing.

I remember when I began to dig into the Bible. It began transforming me from the start. I've often been known to say that Jesus saved my soul, but the Word of God saved my mind. I'd had no alternative but to believe all I had grown up thinking, but when I began discovering in the Word that all I thought wasn't necessarily true, I began changing my mind. And changing my mind changed my life. I'm so glad Jesus didn't come just to save my soul but to save all of me.

I find it encouraging that in the early days of Jesus' ministry, He began with a public proclamation: "Repent, because the kingdom of heaven has come near." The Greek word for "repent" is *metanoia*, which means "to change one's mind."[21] It's like Jesus began His ministry saying, "Hey, it's time to change your mind. Repent. You need to think a different way."

Isn't that the gift He's given me? And you? The freedom and power and ability to change our minds? To go from lost to saved? Then from saved to continually being transformed in every area of our lives? What Jesus preached is the way He wants us to live. He wants us saved and He wants us to continue changing our minds, according to what we read and learn from the Word of God, so we think more like Him. So we can exchange what we've been thinking for His thoughts and endure in a life of faith with strength, moving through things with His perspective—with the mind of Christ.

Have you changed your mind lately? Have you had a rethink about a particular perspective? Have you opened the Word of God and then opened your mind to align your thoughts with God's thoughts?

Remember what Jesus said. Be willing to change your mind—according to the Word—because there's nothing more powerful than a changed mind.

Jesus, please help me repent in the way You meant. Help me learn and grow from Your Word and change my mind. Help me think Your thoughts and not my own. In Your name, amen.

44 AN INSIDE JOB

But godliness with contentment is great gain. For we brought nothing into the world, and we can take nothing out. If we have food and clothing, we will be content with these.

1 TIMOTHY 6:6–8

'm pretty good at soldiering on, but I have never had to overcome like Paul did. When he wrote today's verse, he had overcome being imprisoned—three times—and being beaten, stoned, shipwrecked, and adrift at sea. In his journeys he experienced danger in everything from false brothers posing as Christ-followers to robbers on the roadways to exposure and hunger.

And yet what Paul learned in the midst of it all, that he wrote to his protégé Timothy, is the same thing God calls us to learn: to find our contentment in Christ. Paul knew that true contentment did not lie in what he had but in whose he was. He belonged to Jesus, and knowing that gave him contentment.

I'm so glad to know that the great apostle Paul had to learn the art of contentment, because being content has not come easy to me. I have had to participate in the school of life, often learning from my mistakes, to understand how to be content regardless of my circumstances. Maybe it hasn't come easy for you either. We often think that a promotion, or a partner, or a new home, or new car, or more followers on social media will make us content, only to get these and still feel empty on the inside. It's in those moments we realize that things and people and circumstances cannot bring us true, long-lasting contentment. Only God can do that—and only when we lean into Him to fill the longings of our hearts.

When we lean into God, it is the Holy Spirit who works in us, teaching us how to live contentedly. So we can live in peace. So we can endure. When we learn to cultivate deep-down contentment, we discover a life of more joy and greater peace of mind, regardless of what's happening around us. We understand that although a vacation, a promotion, or a new house and good friends are great gifts, they cannot give us what we ultimately need.

Are you ready for more contentment in your life? More peace of mind? More joy? Discovering that it has everything to do with what is going on inside you, and not anywhere else, is key. Look inside and lean into Jesus, because it's always an inside job.

Holy Spirit, teach me to look to God for contentment. Help me find it in my relationship with Jesus, my Savior. Help me not get caught up in what won't sustain me. In Jesus' name, amen.

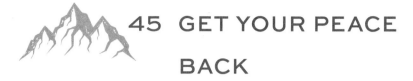

45 GET YOUR PEACE BACK

"Peace I leave with you. My peace I give to you. I do not give to you as the world gives. Don't let your heart be troubled or fearful."
JOHN 14:27

H ave you ever had a phone call, and just by the tone of someone's voice you knew it was not good news? No matter what you were in the middle of, you just knew. It's like the person's extra effort to remain calm and speak in an even tone gave it all away. I remember a time when Nick called me and I could hear the creepy calm in his voice. It was all I could do not to blurt out, "Just say it!" I'm not sure if I held my breath or not, but I did instinctively brace myself for whatever he was about to tell me. When he went on, he explained that he and the girls had been in a wreck, not a serious one, and they were okay. Still, no one wants to get a call like that.

You can imagine the rapid fire of questions I asked: "Are the girls all right? Are you sure? Do they need to be checked out by a doctor? Are you sure? Are you okay? Are you sure?" I know Nick was glad when I stopped drilling him. It just came out of me. I'm a wife and mother before all else. Of course I'm going to ask serious questions and nonsensical ones, all at the same time. Besides, I'm Greek on top of all that.

He and the girls were indeed fine, but, as you can imagine, it was my peace of mind that went first. Isn't that the way it always is? The good news is, as fast as it went, I got it back. As fast as my heart started racing and my questions started flying, I turned to Jesus. I leaned into Him. I put all my trust in Him. I put my family in His hands once more.

I have learned through the years how important it is to not let my heart be troubled or fearful—and how essential my peace of mind is. At times it is the strength I need to get through situations. And at times it's more important than answers. Sometimes we think answers will give us peace, but real peace—the kind Jesus gives—is ours whether we have answers or not.

I have come to understand that peace, the kind that Jesus bought and paid for us, is not the absence of problems but the presence of Jesus Himself. Isn't that what He reassured His disciples before He left this earth? "Peace I leave with you. My peace I give you."

Is your heart troubled today? Is fear overtaking you? What has robbed you of your peace? Whether it was a phone call, an accident, a diagnosis, a breakup, a financial loss, or something else entirely, turn to Jesus. Lean into Him. Put your trust in Him once more. Get your peace back. It's a critical component to your enduring in your life of faith.

Jesus, through You I have peace with God, and I have the peace of God. Please show me how to keep my peace, especially when life tries to take it away from me. In Your name, amen.

46 DRIVE OUT THE FEAR

There is no fear in love; instead, perfect love drives out fear, because fear involves punishment. So the one who fears is not complete in love.

1 JOHN 4:18

W hen we first moved to the States, someone gave our family tickets to Disneyland. For Catherine and Sophia, getting to meet Mickey was the opportunity of a lifetime. The four of us made a day of it, covering as much of the park as we could. To keep Catherine from getting bored, Nick took her on the bigger rides, while Sophia and I spent most of the morning riding everything under two miles per hour, which included rides like Peter Pan's Flight and Dumbo the Flying Elephant. In fact, we rode those rides, and a number of others, multiple times. Once Sophia got over any initial hesitation regarding a ride, she couldn't go enough, so we'd no sooner get off than we'd get back in line and go for another turn. It was fun to watch her realize that there really wasn't anything to fear. Still, she was not interested in riding anything too fast and furious, which was fine with me. I'm pretty low-key when it comes to fast rides anyway.

After lunch we walked past a kiddie roller coaster, and to my surprise, Sophia asked to ride. If she were older and more experienced this wouldn't have been any big deal, but Sophia had never been on a roller coaster. I couldn't help feeling proud of her for wanting to, but at the same time I was concerned. If you're a mother you know the tension of moments like that. All I could think is that we'd go all the way through the line, get on board, and she'd start having a meltdown and want off, and then I would have to flag the attendant down to help us. Or worse, it would start moving and I would have a hysterical kid on my hands for the duration.

I remember staring at Sophia, trying to comprehend what she was suggesting while living out scenarios in my head. I wasn't all that willing to let her do it until I realized she wanted to ride so she could overcome her fear of riding. Well, that changed everything.

As we stood in line, I did my best to build her courage. I reminded her that fear wasn't from God. That perfect love drives out fear. That we have the mind of Christ.[22] By the time we boarded I could see both fear and faith in her, but she was determined to go through with it. She took all the curves and downhill drops like a champ. I was so proud of her. Sometimes the only way to overcome fear is to face it. To do it afraid. To endure in faith in spite of the fear. Every time God asks me to step into something new, I feel like Sophia did. I am full of faith, but that doesn't mean I don't feel afraid at the same time. Still, I don't let that stop me.

Are you facing something that makes you feel afraid? Don't let that stop you. Keep moving forward. Lean into the love of Jesus, and as you're moving, His love will drive out all the fear.

Jesus, I lean into You and Your love today. Help me keep moving forward, renewing my mind with Your truth, so I can keep overcoming the fear that comes against me. In Your name, amen.

47 GOD WILL SEE US THROUGH

Jonathan said to the attendant who carried his weapons, "Come on, let's cross over to the garrison of these uncircumcised men. Perhaps the LORD will help us. Nothing can keep the LORD from saving, whether by many or by few." His armor-bearer responded, "Do what is in your heart. Go ahead! I'm completely with you."

1 SAMUEL 14:6-7

I was never encouraged to take risks when I was growing up. Safety, security, predictability, and comfort were values celebrated in our home. Perhaps because my parents had to flee Egypt because of political unrest when they were just teenagers, they had experienced enough adventure to last them a lifetime. If I expressed a desire to try something new, make new friends, or visit a new place, I was quickly dismissed and discouraged from pursuing these things.

Over time, to maintain the status quo at home, I learned to stay in the box that was created for me. But when I became a Jesus-follower, something inside me changed. I knew He had invited me to a faith adventure, and I could not fulfill my purpose and stay within the confines of my culture and tradition at the same time.

As terrifying as it was, I was going to have to disappoint some people in order to obey God. I was going to have to step out of the boat, take some risks, and trust Jesus.

When people look at my life today, it's hard for them to believe I came from such a rigid, risk-averse background. Jesus has led me to help rescue the victims of human trafficking and to equip and empower people all over the world to fulfill their God-given purpose. Surely I must have had a certain personality type that was given to taking risks. Surely I knew where Jesus was leading me every step of the way. Surely I get an adrenaline rush from being involved in dangerous things. Right? Absolutely not.

When I said yes to Jesus, and every time I say yes to an assignment I believe He has called me to, I feel more like Jonathan in the story surrounding today's verse. I often repeat his very words to our team: "Perhaps the Lord will help us." I'd love to say I have had angelic visitations clearly outlining God's plan for my life, but I have not. It has been more of a case of stepping out in faith to find out if God is in it. That "perhaps" He will help us.

I think one of the greatest keys to long-term endurance is to be willing to live in the "perhaps" realm. If we are waiting for sixteen confirmations from God and three visitations from angels dancing on our beds before we do anything, we will never do anything. The life of faith is a life of risks. If we miss it or make a mistake, God is big enough to get us back on track if our hearts are open and willing.

Heavenly Father, please continue to renew my mind to think like You, to see life from Your perspective, to be willing to live in the "perhaps" realm and trust You more. In Jesus' name, amen.

48 MOVE FORWARD
WITH HIM

"Enlarge the site of your tent, and let your tent curtains be stretched out; do not hold back; lengthen your ropes, and drive your pegs deep."
ISAIAH 54:2

When I was pregnant for the first time, I remember when I suddenly could no longer fit in my clothes. It seemed like it happened overnight. One day my pants met in the middle and the next they didn't. As the months went by and Catherine grew inside of me, I was amazed at how my body kept making room for her. Near the end, when I didn't think I could stretch any more, I did. My body did whatever it had to do to accommodate her. It felt like everything had been rearranged inside me. When my due date finally arrived, I couldn't wait to have her—and it wasn't just because I wanted to hold her in my arms. I was ready to get back to the fitness activities I'd enjoyed before pregnancy.

When I think of what I went through, I can't help but see how God's plans and purposes grow on the inside of us—much like a baby does. When Catherine was inside me, no bigger than a grain of rice, all her potential was there from the beginning. But she had to grow. So it is with us. From the time we gave our lives to Jesus, all our potential has been on the inside of us. It's as though God placed all His thoughts and ideas and dreams for us inside us, and then He said to us, much like He said to the children of Israel, "I can't fit what I want to do in your life in the space you have. I need you to make more room. Enlarge your tent (figuratively speaking)." And then He started helping us stretch—spiritually.

We don't typically live in tents like the children of Israel did, and God's not telling us to move into one and make it as big as possible, but He is telling us to go further internally—to go deeper with Him. To lengthen and strengthen our relationship with Him. To enlarge. To stretch. But not just once. He wants us to be doing this all throughout our lives.

So many times when He's led me to stretch, it's as though I have felt Him challenging me to imagine more, dream more, think bigger, pray to reach more people. After more than three decades of this kind of stretching I've come to understand that all His plans and purposes for me were there at the beginning, but I was not big enough back then to do any of them. I had to grow where He wanted me to go. I had to grow in knowledge and wisdom. I had to get out of my comfort zone again and again. I had to learn new skills. I had to stay teachable. I had to be willing to renew my mind and think according to what the Word says. I had to go through some places that challenged me spiritually and helped me build endurance so I could go the distance.

What about you? Have you ever felt God wanting you to stretch? Did you see how it was related to the potential He'd put inside you? Maybe it was connected to a dream. An idea. A passion. Keep enlarging your tent—stretching, learning, growing, and moving forward with Him.

Heavenly Father, help me to grow where You want me to go. Help me stretch, learn, and keep changing my mind to think more like You. I want to go the distance. In Jesus' name, amen.

49 RIGHT HERE, RIGHT NOW

As for you, exercise self-control in everything, endure hardship, do the work of an evangelist, fulfill your ministry.

2 TIMOTHY 4:5

A re we there yet?" It's a question every parent has answered at least once, right? When we've taken road trips, it's been amazing to me how quickly Catherine and Sophia tire of the drive and start asking the proverbial question. Of course, being the person who likes to get everywhere I'm going as quickly as possible, I may be thinking it right along with them, but I know better than to voice it. After all, we'll get there when we get there.

I wish I were as patient in every area of my life, but like you, I've had to develop patience. And nowhere do I practice it more than in getting to the dreams and initiatives God has dropped into my heart. It can be so frustrating to know what God wants us to do but feel at a loss as to how to get there. To feel helpless to speed up the process. To want to get things done. We're "here"—wherever our "here" is—and we just want to be "there," which is somewhere further down the road than where we are.

This is why I find today's verse so encouraging. I appreciate its context. Paul was at the finish line of his life. He had run his race. He had endured and fought the good fight of faith. And now he was looking back, coaching his protégé, Timothy. His final words make it clear he was on the threshold between what was going on in him "here" as he prepared for arriving "there."

Paul's final journey was the same one he'd been on all along. It was the same one Timothy was traveling. And it's the same one we trek. We're always on our way from "here" to "there" in some area of our lives. And what is a "here" in our lives was once someone else's "there." What is "there" in our lives was once someone else's "here." Are you following this? Like Paul and Timothy, there's always someone on the road behind us and someone on the road ahead of us. We need to focus on doing the work we've been called to do in every moment of our journeys.

It's so easy to slip into the "Are we there yet?" mind-set. To constantly think about where we're not yet. What we've not attained yet. What we have yet to acquire. To be so focused "there," we miss all the "here." What if we took today to just be present in the here and now? And to give our "there" to God? I think it would free up our hearts and minds to be at peace. To be content. To endure in faith. Besides, we only have right now. No matter how far we travel, the only place we'll ever really be is "here," because even when we reach the next "there," it will become our next "here." "Right here, right now"—let that be what you tell yourself each day.

Heavenly Father, please help me remember to be right here, right now, all day today and every day. Help me recognize the value in every moment and live it for You. In Jesus' name, amen.

50 LEARN TO BE CONTENT

I don't say this out of need, for I have learned to be content in whatever circumstances I find myself.

PHILIPPIANS 4:11

Traveling like I do, I sometimes find myself adjusting to a different time zone and being wide awake at 2:00 a.m. Sometimes I've watched TV to try and make myself sleepy, though I don't usually find many options in the middle of the night. Streaming my favorite shows on my laptop is definitely more ideal, but there have been times when I've resorted to watching one of those shopping networks. The ones where they sell everything from easy egg crackers to miracle wrinkle creams to the latest juicer. It never ceases to amaze me how many ways they work to sell you something you've never needed before.

What strikes me the most is how they can take inanimate objects and convince me I might need one. With the easy egg cracker (which, trust me, it's an actual thing), I felt inspired that I might cook more. And when they promised that if I bought one my life would never be the same, and then a celebrity promoted it, it grew even harder to resist. All my life I had been content to crack open eggs with my hands until one infomercial disrupted my bliss and made me discontent.

I hope you're laughing, but isn't that basically how we're bombarded every day of our lives? Isn't there something always trying to sow seeds of discontent in our hearts and minds? Something that makes us think that true contentment is just out of reach? Why is it that we can be perfectly content with our own kitchen until we see someone else's? Or we think our vacation was the best until we see someone else's on social media—albeit cropped, edited, and filtered. It's like the power of suggestion steals our peace.

Living on a never-ending quest for something better can lead to a life of discontent. Of never living with peace in our hearts and minds. Of endless unrest. Surely, from what Paul wrote, this is not what God wants for us. How can we endure in faith if we never have peace?

Everything we think might give us significance and security can only be found in Jesus. True contentment, peace, hope, joy, purpose, and fulfillment can only be found in Him. But none of it comes automatically. Paul wrote that he had learned to be content, which means to be satisfied to the point where we're not disturbed or disquieted.[23] Isn't that what we all desire? It will take effort. We'll have to renew our minds. Change our perspectives. Take on the mind of Christ by filtering everything we think through God's Word. But I'm ready. Are you? Wherever you find yourself today, especially if it's in a place you never expected to land, learn to be content in Jesus. Look to Him for all that your heart yearns for—particularly for His peace.

Heavenly Father, please help me keep my heart and mind on You and all that is mine in Jesus. Help me have peace of mind and contentment in my heart. In Jesus' name, amen.

PART 3

RUNNING OUR RACE
WITH PERSEVERANCE

*Only those who will risk going too far can possibly
find out just how far they can go.*

T. S. ELIOT

51 IN SUCH A WAY

Don't you know that the runners in a stadium all race, but only one receives the prize? Run in such a way to win the prize.

1 CORINTHIANS 9:24

I grew up with parents who were obsessed with our Greek heritage and recounted countless examples of Greek inventions throughout history. From arched bridges to alchemy to surgical instruments to central heating to the Olympics, I grew up hearing about them all. My parents never skipped over a reason to remind my brothers and me why we should be proud to be Greek.

One story I especially appreciate happened in the fourth century BC, when the Greek and Persian army fought in the Battle of Marathon. The Greeks were outnumbered four to one, and it appeared they had no chance of winning. Still, they launched a surprise attack. Shockingly, when it was over, the Greeks had won. The victory inspired the imagination of the Greeks, and a tale was born: a soldier named Pheidippides, who fought in the battle and survived, raced about twenty-five miles all the way back to Athens with the news. The reason I call it a tale is because Pheidippides did run the distance, and what happened after he ran did happen, it's just disputed as to when he actually ran.[24] Either way, it makes today's verse especially significant when it comes to our spiritual race.

As the story goes, he ran at full speed the entire distance and never stopped even once. Historians attain that he was so exhilarated by the victory, pure adrenaline must have kept him going. When he finally entered Athens, he shouted, "We are victorious!" and then he keeled over and died. Literally.

I find it telling that from what historians have said, all Pheidippides needed to do was to hydrate, eat, and rest during his run, and he would have probably lived. His life was cut short because he ran a marathon more like a sprint, and the consequences were inevitable. In the same way, if you and I are going to run in such a way that we will obtain the prize, we must ensure that we do not run out of steam prematurely due to running in a way that is antithetical to building strength, endurance, and perseverance into our spiritual muscles. Let's pace ourselves by ensuring we rest, renew, replenish, and recharge regularly.

I can't help but think of how Paul said, "Run in such a way to win the prize." How are you running your race? Let's be sure to run our race "in such a way" that we obtain the prize.

Jesus, help me run my race in such a way that I reach the finish line having become all that You created me to become and having done all that You created me to do. In Your name, amen.

52 AN IMPERISHABLE CROWN

Now everyone who competes exercises self-control in everything. They do it to receive a perishable crown, but we an imperishable crown.

1 CORINTHIANS 9:25

A t the beginning of the pandemic in 2020, when we were first locked down, I unexpectedly had more downtime than usual. For someone who was used to traveling most days a year, coming to a screeching halt was an adjustment. I remember praying one day and telling the Lord how I wanted to be sure and use this unexpected hiatus wisely.

Part of my strategy for making the most of the time included going through every box in our garage and cleaning out the clutter. It had been a decade since we'd moved in, and from the day we unloaded, we were on the go. I think we only sorted what was most essential and the rest got neatly stacked out of sight.

I'm not sure everyone in our family shared my enthusiasm for cleaning out the garage, but it didn't take long before we were caught up laughing at all we discovered. One box of memories I opened was filled with all the trophies, medals, and ribbons I had won throughout high school and college. It was quite a collection of awards for netball, table tennis, soccer, and various academic achievements. Some were forty years old, and most were damaged, broken, or faded. My name had even come off some of them. How important they had all once been to me, lined up in rows on shelves in my childhood bedroom. There was actually a time when I was so passionate about table tennis, I almost made it to the Olympics. Now my trophies were piled in a box, long forgotten. Every honor I came across was a good reminder that temporal accolades come and go, but our eternal rewards last for eternity. Persevering and being faithful to Jesus in this life is what yields eternal rewards that don't crumble or perish like my trophies.

Paul said everyone competes to receive a perishable crown—like the awards I won so many years ago—but we run our spiritual race on this earth to receive an imperishable one. An eternal one. I understand that this race we're running sometimes gets so hard that it's difficult to imagine how to keep moving forward, but persevering is what results in the eternal rewards we long for. That's why every step of our race matters. Our purpose matters. The plans God has for us matter. How important then that we run our race in such a way that we not only cross the finish line but receive an imperishable crown.

Heavenly Father, please help me run my race the way Paul said, for an imperishable crown. Help me remember that the accolades I receive in this life are temporal, but Your eternal rewards last forever. In Jesus' name, amen.

53 JUST GETTING WARMED UP

As you see, the LORD has kept me [Caleb] alive these forty-five years as he promised. . . . Here I am today, eighty-five years old. I am still as strong today as I was the day Moses sent me out. My strength for battle and for daily tasks is now as it was then. Now give me this hill country the LORD promised me on that day.

JOSHUA 14:10–12

The internship program at A21, the anti-human-trafficking organization Nick and I founded, is one of my favorite ways we invite people to be a part of the work we do. There's nothing like an office full of college-age students who are full of passion, zeal, great ideas, and initiatives, ready to make a difference. But a few years ago, when a colleague told me that a grandmother applied to be an intern, I was genuinely surprised. Her name was Laura, and she believed God still had so much more for her life. She did not want to retire, she said; she wanted the second half of her life to be impactful. So, naturally, we couldn't wait to bring her on.

From the start, Laura dove right in as part of the team. She had a huge learning curve when it came to understanding all the technology, but as awkward as it was, she pushed through her discomfort and studied hard—and the millennials on our team rallied around her. They wanted to glean from her years of wisdom and life experiences, and she was ready to pour it out. She was fulfilling her purpose and at the same time giving more purpose to everyone around her. She was a role model showing us that you don't have to stop at any point—that you can keep going, regardless of your age.

Watching her learn from the younger generations—and watching them grow from her wisdom—inspired me. The entire atmosphere of our office shifted because one woman decided that she was going to be strong, tenacious, courageous, resilient, and humble enough to keep persevering. Her wholehearted attitude reminded me so much of Caleb, particularly when he reached eighty-five years old. He had endured. He said he was as strong as he was the day Moses sent him to spy out the promised land, and that his strength for battle and daily tasks was the same—forty-five years later! The kind of spirit that Caleb had is the kind of spirit I want to always have, don't you? One that says, "I'm eighty-five and God isn't finished with me yet." One that says, "There is still kingdom work to be done." One that says, "There are still kingdom assignments to fulfill, and I want a piece of the action. I am still enduring in faith and, until I draw my last breath, I won't be done."

I don't have any way of knowing how old you are, but I do know you are not too old. If you woke up this morning, there's more for you to do. It's not too late to start. That's what Laura was saying to us when she applied to be an intern. That's what Caleb was saying at eighty-five. Like them, you could just be getting started!

Heavenly Father, please help me move forward as wholehearted in my faith as Caleb was, so I can do all the kingdom assignments You have for me. In Jesus' name, amen.

54 RUN WHERE HE WANTS YOU TO GO

Without revelation people run wild, but one who follows divine instruction will be happy.
PROVERBS 29:18

My friend Dawn has run so many marathons, she knows what it takes to train physically, mentally, and nutritionally. She knows what it is to strategically work out and build stamina over the course of years so she can go the distance running the entire 26.2 miles, pacing herself all along the way. As we have hiked mountains together and had so many conversations, I've learned more than I've ever understood about serious runners. Suffice it to say, as much as I enjoy running, I'm definitely not one of them.

As Dawn has shared her experiences with me I have found it intriguing to learn that a classic marathon runner always envisions the entire 26.2 miles of the race from start to finish. Though they can't see every bend and curve physically from the starting point, they familiarize themselves with the route and they know based on their pace where they will be at any given time. Having that vision of the whole race empowers them to anticipate what is ahead—and to persevere to the finish line.

When I read today's verse, it seems similar. The writer of Proverbs told us all that without revelation people run wild. In other words, without a vision, people will perish.[25] When we, as Jesus-followers, have a sense of vision for our spiritual, emotional, physical, relational, and financial life, it helps us to build endurance and persevere to keep running our race. Keeping a long-term perspective and not just a short-term one helps us stay ready for what's ahead. Knowing we still have distance to cover helps us keep going when we encounter momentary setbacks, failures, disappointments, and heartaches. We'll realize that these are not the end of our journey but part of our race.

It's so easy to get stuck along the way—to find ourselves in a season longer than we intended—but vision will keep us going. At every stage of my life, vision for my purpose has kept me showing up on the way to where I was going—on the way to where I believed God was taking me next. I remember how, in the early years of ministry, I wasn't preaching anywhere, but I knew I would someday. So to practice, I would preach to the trees in Lalor Park. I knew there was a whole race in front of me with a start, a middle, and a finish, and I didn't want to get in on the race in the last lap. I started running where I was, enduring and persevering all the way through. Even today, I keep showing up where God has placed me, knowing that I will eventually run to the next place He has for me.

Do you have a vision for your future? If not, ask God to show you what He has in mind. Ask Him how you can start where you are. Then keep running to where He wants you to go.

Father, please show me Your vision for my future. Show me where You want me to go, and I'll keep it in my line of sight. I'll start running right where I am. In Jesus' name, amen.

 # 55 PREPARE FOR THE MARATHON

He [Elisha] turned back from following him [Elijah], took the team of oxen, and slaughtered them. With the oxen's wooden yoke and plow, he cooked the meat and gave it to the people, and they ate. Then he left, followed Elijah, and served him.

1 KINGS 19:21

I have friends who've been running for years, and most all of them have kept every medal and all their racing numbers. If I were them, I feel sure I would too. It's quite an achievement to build the strength and endurance to run any race.

I remember when a friend of mine from Canada wanted to run in the Boston Marathon, one of the longest-running marathons in the world. Once he truly committed, he spent two years getting his mind and body ready for the race. Two years. For serious runners, this kind of commitment is no surprise. They know that if you run a long-distance race without the right preparation, then you will most likely do damage to your body and quite possibly not be able to run again.

For a not-so-serious runner like me, who only dreams of running such a race, I tend to think of this kind of preparation with a spiritual perspective—because I know from years of experience we can't run our race spiritually and go the distance without embracing the years of preparation God has for us. If I had not been faithful to work with youth at a local level, I would not have been prepared to work with youth at a national level. And had I not been prepared there, there would be no A21. There would be no Propel Women, the leadership initiative we designed to celebrate every woman's passion, purpose, and potential. What we do in one season of preparation affects the next. We build strength and muscle in one season that we will need to carry the weight of the next season. There are no incidental seasons in the stages of perseverance. Even when we think nothing is happening, God is always doing something and preparing us for what He has prepared for us.

I see this in today's verse; the last sentence is an indication of the beginning of a season of preparation—one that lasted years—for Elisha. Elisha served Elijah, and Elijah mentored him. By the time Elijah took off his mantle and went up to heaven, Elisha was ready. When the time came, he picked up Elijah's mantle and put it on.[26]

What has God put in your heart to do? The endurance and perseverance you will need requires a skill set that can only be built with preparation—and the degree to which you commit to the preparation will determine how much of your race you will run and finish. If you bypass any of the preparation, you may get to run a quick sprint, but you won't have the necessary muscles developed to finish the long-distance race you've been called to run. Let's commit together to prepare for all God has for us and run our race well. Then we can meet up at the finish line and celebrate. I'll see you there.

Heavenly Father, thank You for the years of preparation in my life. Please help me stay committed and embrace the testing, training, and strengthening. In Jesus name, amen.

56 FROM START TO FINISH

I discipline my body and bring it under strict control, so that after preaching to others, I myself will not be disqualified.

1 CORINTHIANS 9:27

When I first began hiking with Dawn, I did my best to buy the right equipment. I listened to everything she coached me to consider, and I read countless reviews on what fellow hikers said worked for them and what didn't. Still, nothing prevented the normal aches and pains that came with pushing my fifty-plus-year-old knees up a mountain. I've had aching joints, sore muscles, powerful cramps, sore feet, a back that hurt at the end of the day, and on I could go. But it's all part of the process. If you want to push your body to do something new, it's going to hurt. There will be resistance.

I've had to learn that to finish any trail I start I have to press past the pain barrier. I have to go beyond the inevitable mental and physical wall I'm likely to hit and endure the discomfort. To reach the goal of taking in the view at the summit—to experience all the thrill—and then get all the way back down, I will have to pay the price of the pain.

Have I inspired you to start trekking mountains with me yet? As challenging as it can be, I promise, it's still totally worth it. From the wildlife to the forest to the wildflowers to the breathtaking views—to the feeling that you're growing in strength in ways you never imagined you could. For me, there's just nothing that compares.

Still, I can't deny there have been times on the mountain when I wanted to quit and when I was in so much pain I thought I would have to. More than once, I have envisioned myself calling Nick and having him call the rescue helicopter to come for me, but then I always remember I didn't start this not to finish.

I have found that hiking is just like everything else in my life. Whatever I feel God leading me to do, if I start it, I want to finish it regardless of the pain threshold. It's the same sense I get when I read about Paul and his journeys. They inspire me to keep pushing through, no matter how hard it gets. In today's verse, Paul said that he disciplined his body. Another translation says he disciplined it by hardships and subdued it, for fear he would find himself unfit, not standing the test, unapproved and rejected as a counterfeit.[27] Can you imagine? After all Paul went through on this earth, he still feared falling short. If Paul could feel that way, it's no wonder he endured whatever discomfort he had to in order to finish his race on this earth.

What about you? How's your race going? Are you facing an uphill climb today? Set your heart and mind to persevere. Let all the endurance you've been building fuel you to keep on running strong—to go the distance from start to finish.

Father, help me press past the pain barrier, to go beyond the inevitable walls I encounter. Help me to persevere and to let endurance keep me running strong. In Jesus' name, amen.

57 MAKE EVERY EFFORT

Not that I have already reached the goal or am already perfect, but I make every effort to take hold of it because I also have been taken hold of by Christ Jesus.

PHILIPPIANS 3:12

O nce, when I was running in Thessaloniki, Greece, the city where we opened our first A21 office years ago, I got lost. To this day I'm not sure how, but I got turned around and went right when I should have gone left. By the time I realized that nothing looked familiar, I was miles away from where I'd started. I found myself at an intersection, reading street signs, trying to figure out where I had gone wrong, mentally retracing my steps, and wondering, *How did I get here?*

Grateful that it was still daylight, since I'd started out early in the afternoon, I began thinking through the position of the sun and imaging the layout of the city so I could determine in which direction I could find the harbor. I knew the heights of the upper city were to the north, and the harbor was to the south. And right before the harbor was Aristotelous Square, one of the best-known landmarks in the city. My hotel was between the heights and the square. If I could figure out which direction to go to find one of them, I could make my way back. When I had my bearings I took off in hopes I was right.

More than once I wanted to give up. I grew tired. My tummy rumbled as I smelled amazing food wafting from all the tavernas. I would have stopped for a bite, but I hadn't brought my wallet. My leg cramped. I doubted my inner compass. Still, there was no way to get back other than to keep running. Block after block, I pressed on, making it back a full hour later than I had planned—but only because I had built up endurance from years of running.

Isn't this how endurance and perseverance work in our spiritual lives too? Just as we have to make every effort and press on in spite of physical discomfort—like I did when I was running—we have to press on spiritually through whatever might be pressing on us. Don't we have to make every effort, as Paul said? I think so.

Paul said he had not yet reached the goal, nor was he already perfect, but he continued to make every effort. He continued to press on, as one of my favorite translations says.[28]

If we're going to run our race in such a way that we make it across the finish line, having fulfilled all the plans and purposes God prepared for us, then we will have to make every effort. We will have to press through everything that is pressing on us and against us. I know from the pain of experience that it won't be easy, but, in Christ, we can do it. We can press on.

Jesus, help me press through everything that is pressing on me and against me. Help me to keep enduring in faith, moving forward, doing all that You planned for me. In Your name, amen.

58 THE MAIN THING

I pursue as my goal the prize promised by God's heavenly call in Christ Jesus.
PHILIPPIANS 3:14

When Paul wrote today's declaration, he had already survived imprisonment and being stoned, shipwrecked, and adrift at sea. Can you imagine? If it were me, I would be asking God to give me a villa in Santorini. I'd be suggesting that perhaps I needed to take a break after taking so much for the team. But not Paul. He pressed on for the prize, which is Jesus.

Understanding all he went through and that he still endured in his faith makes his words mean so much. It helps them become an anthem we can hang on to, especially when life is hard. I have seen this in my friends who have lost spouses, lost children, lost marriages. I've watched them grieve and yet find a way to keep moving forward, and I've wondered more than once, *How do they keep going?* Deep down I know the answer because I see how they love Jesus. I see how they have built endurance in their lives by continually pursuing the prize, like Paul did, even when they are in pain and moving through what they never thought they would have to move through. And to be honest, when I look at my own life, I see how I've done the same in trying times.

But what's interesting and puzzling and frustrating, all at the same time, are the moments when I have been facing something not quite so serious and I've inadvertently given in to the pressure of whatever was pressing in on me. When I've let go of pursuing the prize. As much as I don't like to admit it, there have been many times when I have temporarily taken my eyes off Jesus and given my focus to whatever is attempting to push me over the edge—and typically it was some mundane, everyday thing.

In other words, there have been times when I've made a big deal out of what's not really a big deal. I am aware enough to know that I can be full-on when it would be better to relax a bit. I'm still learning, but what I want to do is pause more and put things into a clearer perspective. Whether it is the smoke detector malfunctioning in the middle of the night that's making me teeter on the edge, or being late to pick up Sophia from school, or having a flight delayed, I continually want to get better at reframing the situations I encounter. I want to see such everyday inconveniences for what they are—inconveniences. I want to put them into a perspective that values perseverance, living my life on mission, building endurance, and pressing on for the prize. I want to move through my life seeing every situation through a lens like the one Paul saw through. He managed to keep the main thing the main thing.

Let's work on this together. Let's go before the throne of God and evaluate our inconveniences today. Let's shrink them back down to size. Let's keep the main thing the main thing—persevering in our pursuit of the prize: Jesus.

Jesus, please help me keep my eyes on You and not on all the inconveniences I encounter today. Please help me keep the main thing the main thing—pursuing You. In Your name, amen.

59 FOCUS ON YOUR WHY

I consider my life of no value to myself; my purpose is to finish my course and the ministry I received from the Lord Jesus, to testify to the gospel of God's grace.

ACTS 20:24

Kylie is my oldest and dearest friend, and like so many of my friends, she frequently runs in marathon races. I am not sure if I am living vicariously through them, but I seem to have amassed many friends who love to run long distances. One thing I love about Kylie is the fact that she follows the same ritual in every marathon race she enters. As soon as the starting gun fires, she says aloud, "Kylie, all you have to do is finish."

Throughout the race, she says this to herself at least one hundred times. She does not try to beat everyone, she does not compare her pace to the speed of everyone else in the race, she simply sets her own pace and runs her race. And most importantly, she wants to get to the finish line.

It's such a great lesson for us all. If our goal is to be conformed and transformed into the image of Jesus, then becoming more like Jesus is our goal. Running our race, the way Jesus wants us to run our race, is our goal. Therefore, we're not out to beat anyone else; we're not out to be better than anyone else; we're doing our best to be more like Jesus.

If we inadvertently get our eyes off the ultimate prize—Jesus—our eyes will fall on other things like people, status, and self-gratification, and we will get off balance and off track. If we take our eyes off the goal, we will quite possibly develop a mentality that things are not moving fast enough. That we're not being rewarded or acknowledged soon enough. And we might even unintentionally uproot ourselves and walk out of our purpose.

To be honest, during some of the greatest challenges of my life and hardest times of ministry—those times when I found myself thinking, *Why am I doing this?* and had twenty legitimate reasons to quit—I've had to get myself refocused on the ultimate goal of when and why God called me. That is what has sustained me in my darkest hours. It's the *why* that helps me keep running when the *how* makes no sense.

Maybe this is where you're wrestling today. Perhaps part of the answer is to refocus on your *why*. More of the answer could be to not get distracted with short-term things that will gratify our immediate wants, so we can finish our course and attain our prize. Let's refocus our eyes and hearts and minds to be on Jesus. Let's purpose to finish our course and the ministry we've received from Jesus, as Luke wrote, so we can testify to the gospel of God's grace.

Jesus, my purpose is to finish my course and the ministry I have received from You. Please help me reach this goal. Help me keep my eyes on You, the ultimate prize. In Your name, amen.

60 KEEP THE FAITH

I am already being poured out as a drink offering, and the time for my departure is close. I have fought the good fight, I have finished the race, I have kept the faith.

2 TIMOTHY 4:6-7

At the 2004 Olympics in Athens, Vanderlei de Lima of Brazil was leading the marathon race, running strong with only three miles to go. Suddenly a crazed man burst onto the track and forcefully grabbed de Lima, pulling him into the crowd. A spectator freed de Lima, and though shaken, de Lima returned to the race. By then he had lost his lead to Italy's Stefano Baldini, and as he pressed on to the goal, he was passed by one other runner. He finished third, winning the bronze medal. At the closing events, de Lima was awarded the Pierre de Coubertin medal for sportsmanship.[29] Everyone knew that de Lima was a winner because he had not given up.

Inevitably in this life, as we run our race spiritually, difficulties will come, obstacles will block our paths, pitfalls will happen, and surprise attacks will threaten to pull us out of our races, but let's determine together to never give up and never give in. To never quit. Let's determine to be like the apostle Paul when he wrote Timothy, "I have fought the good fight, I have finished the race, I have kept the faith."

Maybe you've lost a loved one and you're trying to learn how to live without them around. Maybe you've lost your job and you're trying to find your footing. Maybe you were passed up for a promotion. Perhaps you were betrayed and someone has left your life. Or it could be you're facing an unexpected illness. Life is full of unplanned hurdles to overcome. Some are bigger than others. Some are more difficult to overcome. Still, God wants us to keep fighting the good fight of faith. He's rooting for us and He wants us to endure. To persevere. So we can finish our race.

Let's not lose sight of the fact that our race matters because it's filled with our purpose, with our calling, with who we are. I understand that you might be feeling weary, defeated, disqualified, disillusioned, discouraged, or discombobulated for any number of reasons. You might feel like you have been under nonstop attack. All the more reason why I want to remind you that you are still here. The devil on his best day cannot take you out on your worst day. If you are alive, you are still in your race, and God wants you to make it across your finish line when your purpose is accomplished. In the meantime, keep running and keep the faith.

Heavenly Father, please help me keep running in faith, overcoming all that I've been through. Help me persevere onward and continue building endurance so I can keep fighting the good fight of faith. In Jesus' name, amen.

61 KEEP DOING GOOD

As for you, brothers and sisters, do not grow weary in doing good.
2 THESSALONIANS 3:13

I stepped out of the car and felt the bitter cold of winter. I had traveled to the border of Greece to visit a camp filled with refugees mostly from Syria—people who had survived a deadly journey on foot and then on rubber boats across the Aegean Sea. I wanted to see firsthand the work of A21 in the camp and gain an understanding of the situation.

Seeing a group of volunteers handing out coats a few yards away, I felt compelled to join them. The line, filled with fathers and mothers and their children, appeared to go on forever. As I began handing out coats I heard a woman shouting on the other side of the fence that had been built around the camp. Turning, I realized she was yelling directly at me.

I didn't understand her Arabic, but I didn't have to. I glanced at her two children and understood she was begging for me to give them coats. I gestured that she needed to get in line, but she kept pleading. She wasn't giving up. She was *unyielding. Determined. Pressing in. Seeking what she desperately needed.*

I felt caught between helping those who had waited patiently in line and yielding to her persistent demands. Looking at her, I saw such desperation. She was probably two thousand miles from home. She was alone—unusual for a woman in this part of the world—and had risked her life to get to this point. She had probably spent days not knowing how she would feed her children, her husband killed or missing.

Suddenly, the mother instinct in me empathized with the fierceness of her love. If I had been her, I would have been screaming loudly too, demanding just as much. Feeling the cold through my own jacket, I quickly threw her two coats over the fence. Her eyes thanked me.

That night—more than any other in the years since starting A21—I was grateful we had never given up and quit. That we had not grown weary in doing good. That we had endured in faith. Had we not kept going, I would never have had the opportunity to help this woman and her children.

I've never forgotten that mother, and I share my experience to remind us all that whatever God has called us to do, whatever He has put in our hearts to accomplish, let's keep going to Him for strength so we can endure. You never know who is waiting on the other side of your perseverance.

Father, please give me strength to keep enduring in faith, persevering and pressing through everything that's pressing against me so I can do all that You've called me to do. In Jesus' name, amen.

62 DON'T STOP BEFORE YOU START

Let us not get tired of doing good, for we will reap at the proper time if we don't give up.
GALATIANS 6:9

When Nick and I first began researching the possibility of establishing an anti-trafficking organization, we were given a terminal prognosis: impossible. The feasibility study from the consultants we'd hired used that word ten times in their report. *Ten times.* And opening an office in Thessaloniki, Greece? It was the worst location we could pick, they said. They cited several legitimate reasons, including a lack of laws against human trafficking, the presence of corruption, and shaky economics.

But Thessaloniki was the best European location from which to fight global slavery because it was in the middle of the biggest gateway through which illegal migrants entered Europe. Traffickers knew this route, as it had been used for thousands of years for the slave trade. Even the apostle Paul encountered this heinous crime when he intersected with a slave girl on his way to a place of prayer in the city of Philippi, a mere one hundred miles northeast of Thessaloniki.[30] Just as in biblical times, modern-day traffickers have been preying on innocent victims there for years—luring them from impoverished nations with promises of work and hope for a better life.

Still, I couldn't help but ask myself, *Why would God lead me to do something so impossible?* I felt unqualified. *Who am I to tackle something like this?* I had no idea how to run an anti-human trafficking organization. I had no training. I was the mother of two children under four at the time, living on the other side of the world, already working full time. I was not looking to do something else. Didn't the feasibility report confirm how hopeless this idea was? I felt overwhelmed and weary just thinking about the magnitude of the task ahead.

Looking back, it would have been so easy to stop before we ever really started. But impossible is where God starts, and miracles are what God does, so we began where God starts. It wasn't easy getting A21 up and running, but by the grace of God we moved forward. If we hadn't, we would never be reaping the fruit of transformed lives today.

Maybe you've been there. Maybe God gave you a direction or an idea that by all accounts was impossible, but you knew it was the right thing to do. Maybe it was to start an initiative like we did, or a business, or an outreach. Starting anything is work, and it takes endurance to keep going when it looks impossible, doesn't it?

What has God nudged you to do? What is it that you think about from time to time that you know is Him? Don't stop before you start. Persevere in faith and trust Him to show you the next step. Trust Him and His promise that you will reap at the proper time, all because you didn't give up.

Heavenly Father, please help me stay strong, persevering in faith. Help me accomplish all that You've called me to do. In Jesus' name, amen.

63 HE WILL BE FOR YOU

"Now go! I will help you speak and I will teach you what to say."
EXODUS 4:12

There seems to be a precedent in the Bible for God using people who consider themselves unsuitable for a particular task, but when they obeyed and did what He called them to do, whatever they lacked ensured that God received all the glory. Isn't this how it was with Moses?

When God called Moses to go before Pharaoh, the highest person in the land, and demand the Israelites be released from slavery, Moses gave God reasons why someone else might be more qualified—including that he was not eloquent in speech. Rather than let him off the hook, God said, "I will help you speak and I will teach you what to say."

When God began asking me to start the work of A21, to help rescue people enslaved in human trafficking around the world, I could feel Moses' pain. Although I had experience teaching and sharing my testimony, I had never spoken to people about human trafficking. In fact, I felt entirely inadequate to do so. I did not know the right terms to use, nor did I have the right education to qualify me for this type of work. How could someone like me speak to law enforcement, government, community groups, or the media about slavery? I totally felt like Moses going before Pharaoh, and I wanted God to pick someone else.

I found myself wrestling with God and feeling so unsure. Then God showed me in His Word what He made clear to Moses—that who Moses was wasn't as important as who was with him. It helped me see that my insecurities didn't matter any more to God than Moses' insecurities did. What mattered was who was with me, and who had called me, and that was God Himself.

I'll never forget how faith and courage and endurance rose up inside me. I still didn't know how we were going to do it, but I knew we were. And that was enough to help me persevere. It was daunting and overwhelming at times, but God was with me every step of the way.

What has God called you to do? What purpose has He placed in your heart to fulfill? My guess is that you can relate to Moses' fears and concerns just as I did. Maybe you feel just as inadequate or unqualified or insecure. I have found that in every endeavor God has called me to, such feelings are perfectly normal. Who hasn't felt anxious to take on something new, something unknown, something for which we might have no training?

When we trust God and persevere despite our fears, He is faithful to be there. He was for Moses, He was for me, and He will be for you.

Heavenly Father, please help me grow in intimacy with You, trusting You to be there for me as I persevere and move forward in faith. In Jesus' name, amen.

64 RIGHT WHERE WE'RE SUPPOSED TO BE

Moses and Aaron went in to Pharaoh and did just as the LORD had commanded. Aaron threw down his staff before Pharaoh and his officials, and it became a serpent. But then Pharaoh called the wise men and sorcerers—the magicians of Egypt, and they also did the same thing by their occult practices. Each one threw down his staff, and it became a serpent. But Aaron's staff swallowed their staffs.

EXODUS 7:10–12

C an you imagine being in Moses' shoes? He was a man who, while fighting his own fear, agreed to obey God and go before Pharaoh, the most powerful man in the land, and demand the Hebrew slaves be freed. But all it had led to was making life even more difficult for the Hebrew slaves. Two chapters before today's verse, the Bible says that Pharaoh's heart hardened, and he ordered the captives to keep making bricks for his kingdom, only without straw, a necessity for brickmaking.

Now Moses was standing before Pharaoh once again, only this time with his brother, Aaron. In continued obedience to God, Moses was making his demands, trusting God to show up with His power, when suddenly Pharaoh's magicians showed off a power that was seemingly equal to God's. Their staffs turned into snakes too. How could that happen? Instead of things getting better, they only grew worse.

Still, Moses persisted. Over the course of several more visits, Moses appealed to Pharaoh to reverse his decision and let the Hebrew people go. With each visit, Moses had to continue to set aside his fears, his insecurities, his feelings of being unqualified. Each time Pharaoh's heart hardened, and each time God struck the land with a plague.

But Moses persevered. He had an assignment. Despite the fear, the opposition, the hardship, the seeming lack of success, Moses pressed on. He stayed with it, enduring in faith.

I want to have the faith, courage, and perseverance of Moses. I feel sure you do too, but we both know it's not easy. Often, when things get worse before they get better, harder before easier, darker before lighter, we doubt. We doubt God. We doubt our calling. We second-guess ourselves. *Maybe He didn't open that door. Maybe He didn't call me. Maybe this isn't His will.*

God wants us to trust Him even when nothing looks like we had hoped. In my own walk, I have learned that closed doors do not necessarily mean that God is not opening a different way. The presence of a battle does not mean the absence of God in the war. Trials don't mean we are out of the will of God. In fact, they often mean we are precisely in the center of God's will—right where we're supposed to be, doing exactly what we're supposed to be doing.

Heavenly Father, please help me remember that in everything You've called me to do, You are with me, and because of that I can persevere in faith. In Jesus' name, amen.

65 LITTLE BY LITTLE

"I will not drive them out ahead of you in a single year; otherwise, the land would become desolate, and wild animals would multiply against you. I will drive them out little by little ahead of you until you have become numerous and take possession of the land."

EXODUS 23:29–30

H ave you ever noticed that God often seems to be doing a work in us at the same time He's getting us from where we are to where He wants us to go? I have found that He wants us to grow in our character, develop the fruit of the Spirit, and exercise our faith as we make our way from point A to point B. And He typically leads us forward through small, incremental steps instead of giant leaps. Frustrating, I know.

When the children of Israel finally did arrive in the promised land, God wouldn't let them go in to possess all the land immediately. Instead, God worked a very deliberate, step-by-step plan. In today's verse, we read where He told them He would not drive out the inhabitants in a single year; rather, He said He would do it little by little—and that's what He did through them.

God's directive displayed His infinite wisdom and vision for their future. While they were weary of waiting and wanting to rush right in, God knew they couldn't yet manage all that real estate. He knew that in their current condition, the land they desperately wanted—the land He had promised them—had the power to destroy them. They needed to grow stronger first, even after all those years sojourning across the desert, so He put them on a strength-training plan. In the process, He prepared the land for them and prepared them for the land.

Sound familiar? In my own life, I have learned that even though God put a desire in my heart to serve Him when I first became a follower of Christ, I was not ready *then* for all the initiatives I lead *now*. He had to lead me little by little. I needed to learn, grow, change, and develop the muscles of courage, faith, faithfulness, and endurance. These do not grow overnight. This same principle applies to building healthy marriages, friendships, finances, careers, and lifestyles. Most things in life happen little by little. If we are constantly searching for the big advances, we will become frustrated and give up. Look for the little incremental steps and praise Jesus along the way.

What about you? Where is He taking you? It would be so wonderful to accomplish it all quickly, but that most likely won't happen. Instead, you will have to persevere, moving forward step by step, little by little, dependent on Him, letting Him prepare you for the future He's prepared for you.

Heavenly Father, please keep leading me little by little, moving forward, dependent on You, being prepared for all You have prepared for me. Help me trust You more. In Jesus' name, amen.

66 YOU'LL GET TO YOUR THERE

It is precept upon precept, precept upon precept, line upon line, line upon line, here a little, there a little.

ISAIAH 28:10 ESV

Staring into the dark, I couldn't deny the doubts that had begun to creep into my heart or the tears that slipped onto my pillow. The ones that made me wonder if I had made a wrong decision, if I was in the wrong place, if I wasn't really making a difference. I was in my early twenties, working with youth, traveling from one country town to the next. I was speaking in homes, local gymnasiums, and ball fields. I was staying with families who graciously offered me their couch or spare bedroom. And all I could hear was my mum's voice in my head: *Christina, you're wasting your life. How can you live like this? How will you ever get married? You resigned from a corporate job and salary package with incredible benefits for this? Besides all that, a girl has no business driving hours and hours on desolate roads all alone.*

Mum meant well. Her questions were valid, motherly, logical concerns. But despite my tears and doubts, I knew deep down what I was doing was right. I knew the desire God had put in my heart. Still, it was hard. Today's verse reminds us that God has a particular way in which He builds our lives. His method is line upon line and little by little. Most of us would prefer to skip a few lines and gain the promises of God for our lives all at once, but God is more concerned about what is happening in us than through us. He knows that we cannot handle everything all at once, and the process is as important as the destination.

What I didn't understand in my early years of ministry was that God was orchestrating *my* journey for *my* future. He knew that years into the future I would launch initiatives using the very skills I was learning. He knew all my future assignments, and He was preparing me. Now that I'm decades beyond that night, I see it as a place that is familiar to us all. Whether you're an aspiring professional paying your dues, a student toughing out a boring job, or a mom who has paused her career to spend her days changing diapers, we all have rough nights when we doubt our decisions, wondering if we heard God clearly and if it's worth it to keep persevering in faith.

Maybe last night was that night for you. Keep trusting Him. Be patient with His ways of moving you forward little by little. Keep trusting God that He's preparing you for what He's prepared for you. That He knows what's on the road ahead. Let Him keep building endurance in you, a little here and a little there. If you will, then He'll make sure you get to your there.

Father, please help me to trust You more. To stay the course in everything You've called me to do. To persevere, moving forward for Your good and Your glory. In Jesus' name, amen.

67 HE'S GONE
BEFORE YOU

In spite of this you did not trust the LORD your God, who went before you on the journey to seek out a place for you to camp. He went in the fire by night and in the cloud by day to guide you on the road you were to travel.

DEUTERONOMY 1:32–33

Years ago, when I stepped into ministry, I had well-meaning friends question what I was doing. They cared for me, knew the opportunities I had in the corporate world, and wanted to see me succeed—and from their perspective what I was doing didn't make sense. "Christine, what are you doing?" they would ask. "Why are you involved in youth center work? Why are you involved in government? Why are you involved in social justice?" I understood that it made no sense to them, because it didn't always make sense to me. But it made perfect sense to God.

When I was tempted to compare my journey to theirs, especially when they got to where they were going so much faster than I did, I had to fight against discouragement. I had to learn that trusting God includes trusting Him to guide us when we don't quite understand why we are where we are, or how we're going to get to where He has promised.

All these years later, it's the same. If you have a dream, a plan, a purpose, chances are it's going to take time, and the journey might not look anything like you thought. But with each step of faith, we endure, trusting that God is protecting us and preparing us, because He is always for us and never against us.[31] And He's not only *for* us, He's gone on *before* us. Today's verse shows us this. It's a charge read by Moses, leveled against the Israelites, after forty years in the desert and before they entered the promised land. In it Moses reminded the people how God went before them, that He was a fire by night and a cloud by day to guide them.

Isn't that what He's still doing today? To me, the message Moses spoke is clear: God is *always* there to guide us on the road we are to travel. And despite what obstacle we may have to overcome, the real problem we encounter is the same one the Israelites did—we're tempted to stop trusting God. I know for me it's been a lifelong process of stepping out in faith, trusting Him more, sometimes seeing things unfold marvelously and other times experiencing disappointment, all the while persevering and taking the next risk to trust Him again. To endure in faith believing He's still out there before me, guiding me.

What about you? Can you trust that He's gone before you and is protecting you from what you cannot see or aren't yet prepared to handle? Remember, there could be something like a destructive relationship, a toxic work environment, or any number of things on the road ahead. Wherever you are on your path, trust that God has gone before you and He's watching out for you.

Father, please help me trust that You have gone before me, that You are out front guiding me and protecting me from what I cannot see. Help me trust more. In Jesus' name, amen.

68 RUN WITH INTENTION

I do not run like one who runs aimlessly or box like one beating the air.

1 CORINTHIANS 9:26

I imagine we all go through things in this life that cause us to turn on the autopilot and just coast instead of running our race with intention. It's easily understood when we're facing something heartbreaking or disappointing, something that drains the life out of us and throws us off track. But what about when we start coasting because everything is going well? When everything seems to be falling into place instead of falling apart? Have you ever thought about that? Can't that be just as detrimental to how we're running our race?

For some reason, when life is pressing in on us it seems easier to be intentional, but when times are good we tend to relax. It's natural to want to rest and take a breather, and we should. Times of replenishing are necessary to keep running. At the same time, God doesn't want us to get so lax we simply cruise through life. Therein lies a tension we must learn to manage—when to rest and when to run, all the while never simply coasting.

Think about it this way: What do we do when there's no pain in our hearts or pressure bearing down on us from some difficulty? When there's no emergency, no crisis, no challenge? When there's money in the bank, food on the table, and a vacation on the horizon? When we've climbed the professional ladder and work is on the upswing? When we've started the business we've always planned? When our marriage is happy and our kids are well? Or when we're enjoying the single life, perhaps traveling to all the places we've dreamed? Taking the college courses that we have always wanted to take, in the university where we have always hoped to attend?

That's a lot of questions, I know, but the point is, it's all too easy to coast when everything is going great, when we're in a season that is exactly what we prayed for and quite possibly what we worked so hard for.

I find it worthy of our attention that when Paul talked about how he ran his race, he said, "I do not run like one who runs aimlessly." Paul was disciplined. He practiced self-control. He exercised endurance. He ran with intention. And whether times are bad or good, that's how God wants us to run our race too.

If you suspect you've begun to coast, go to Jesus and ask Him to help you renew your focus so you can keep running your race with intention. Ask Him what you can do to keep persevering in faith. All the way to your finish line.

Heavenly Father, please help me keep running my race with intention and not coasting. Help me be mindful with every step, persevering to the finish line. In Jesus' name, amen.

69 FOR WHAT'S ETERNAL

Our momentary light affliction is producing for us an absolutely incomparable eternal weight of glory.

2 CORINTHIANS 4:17

When I was growing up, olive oil was an essential ingredient in Mum's kitchen, and to this day I enjoy a strong and flavorful olive oil on salads, tomatoes, cheese, almost anything. To get flavorful, robust extra virgin olive oil, olives have to be pressed. They have to be crushed. They have to endure being transformed from one state into another. To give you an idea of what I mean, initially, after olives are harvested from the trees, they are quickly cleaned and pressed into a paste, pits and all—either by an ancient method of using a grinding wheel weighing hundreds of pounds or with modern industrial equipment. The paste is then spread onto fibrous cloths that are layered one on top of the other, where they are pressed even more with pounds and pounds of pressure so intense, every drop of oil is squeezed out.

But even after all that, the oil goes through another kind of pressing. It's heated—just high enough but not too high—so the impurities fall to the bottom and the extra virgin olive oil rises to the top. It's silky, beautifully colored, and ready to be stored where it can rest. Later, when it has rested long enough, it is bottled into green or dark-colored glass—the perfect color to block harmful UV rays that can spoil it.

The best-tasting olive oil is made when the olives are picked at just the right time, crushed quickly into a paste, pressed again at just the right intervals, heated to just the right temperature, cooled for just the right amount of time, and then bottled at the right moment. No doubt, to make the perfect bottle of oil requires the right amount of pressing at all the right times.

In similar fashion, for us to persevere in faith, we're going to have to be pressed with the right amount of pressing at all the right times—and then, how well we respond to the pressing will determine how well we endure. In other words, the things we have to press through here on earth have the potential to produce for us an eternal weight of glory. If we want to grow, if we want to become more like Christ, if we want to fulfill all the plans and purposes of God for our lives, we will choose to endure the pressing.

Life is full of pain, suffering, heartache, betrayals, and disappointments. If you are in the midst of one of these today, can I encourage you to see it as a momentary affliction that can actually produce something of eternal value? If you will, I believe you'll find the strength to keep enduring for what's eternal.

Heavenly Father, please help me keep my focus on what is eternal. Help me endure the momentary afflictions that come my way. Help me persevere. In Jesus' name, amen.

70 IT WILL BE WORTH IT

The woman gave birth to a son and named him Samson. The boy grew, and the LORD blessed him. Then the Spirit of the LORD began to stir him in the Camp of Dan, between Zorah and Eshtaol.

JUDGES 13:24–25

Throughout Scripture we see examples of people who had great potential but did not realize the fullness of their purpose—not because they were not gifted, talented, or empowered by God but because they did not pay attention to their inner soul realm. The gift that was on them exceeded the character that was within them, and their lives imploded. That is the sad story of Samson.

Humanly speaking, in Samson's day, no one was physically stronger than he was. He also had spiritual sharpness and mental ability. Even before Samson was born, an angel of the Lord said Samson would begin the deliverance of Israel from the hands of the Philistines.[32] God's hand was on Samson. From today's verse we know that God blessed him and that the Spirit of the Lord stirred in him, but Samson had power without purity. He had strength without self-control. He had an ego that was out of control. He thought he was invincible.

Like Samson, we all have the potential to sabotage our purpose if we do not allow the Holy Spirit to continue to heal us from the inside out. Our inner world totally affects our outer world. For example, if there is a disparity between what is going on inside our hearts and how we are depicting our lives on social media, or at work, or with our family or friends, our worlds will most likely eventually implode—and we won't be able to endure.

By the grace of God, I am still running my race today because over the course of my life I have done some deep work with the Holy Spirit in the realm of my soul. I was so broken after years of abuse and rejection that I have needed deep internal healing on an ongoing basis. I have discovered that the more I have allowed God to do a healing work in my soul, the more He has been able to do through me for His glory. I have come to understand that we all need deep, ongoing work to be conformed and transformed to the image of Christ, so let's determine to embrace it. It is God's grace to us so we will not end up derailing our purpose like Samson did. God is committed to our wholeness, and we must be too.

Invite the Holy Spirit in today to do a healing work. He is tender, gentle, and kind. Let's persevere in becoming all that God created us to be so we can do all that God has called us to do.

Father, please help me understand this realm of the soul in my life and how my inner life affects my outer life. I invite You in to heal all of me. In Jesus' name, amen.

71 TODAY COULD MAKE
ALL THE DIFFERENCE

*Having heard about Jesus, she came up behind him in the crowd and touched
his clothing. For she said, "If I just touch his clothes, I'll be made well."*
MARK 5:27–28

There's a woman in Scripture whose endurance inspires me. I don't know her name, but I do know her story. We often refer to her as the woman with the issue of blood because she was a woman troubled by a ceaseless menstrual cycle. We women can empathize with her physical misery for sure, but what I want us to consider today is how she pressed past what plagued her, even after suffering for twelve years.[33] We know from Scripture that because of her religious culture, she was considered unclean. We know that she had spent all her money on doctors in search of a cure, to no avail.[34] And then one day, Jesus came to her town. That's when she found the motivation, the endurance, the wherewithal to risk leaving her home in search of Him—to press through everything that had been pressing on her.

We can only guess at what went through her mind that day, but if she was anything like most of us when we have suffered through our own trials—perhaps when we've tried everything imaginable to salvage a relationship, redirect a child, bring peace to a family, or survive a diagnosis—I think it safe to imagine the many ways she would have had to persevere. Surely she would have had to press through her own emotions of fear and anxiety. She would have had to press through struggling with whether to take a risk again or with getting her hopes up again. She would have had to be willing to give one more idea, one more remedy, one more possible solution a try—all the while fighting the angst that it might not work. Whether she had to overcome all this, or even some of it, it's astounding that she went for it. She left her house and pressed through the crowds until she found Jesus.

Can you relate to her determination? Her desperation? When she saw Jesus, we know she touched the hem of His clothes and she was healed.[35] She risked pressing in with her faith once more, and once more made all the difference—after twelve long years.

When was the last time you wanted to press in with your faith, but after years of trying you weren't sure you could muster the strength? Maybe today is the day to ask the Holy Spirit to give you the desire to try once again. To press past your past. To press past your fears, your anxiety, or your comfort zone. To press past everything that is pressing on you. To press past your front door, so to speak, and go in search of Jesus. To risk reaching out and touching the hem of His garment. To trust Him once more. Today could be that day that makes all the difference.

Jesus, please help me keep my trust in You no matter how long it takes. Help me remember that You know the desire of my heart and that You've heard my prayers. In Your name, amen.

72 CIRCLE UP YOUR FRIENDS

They came to him bringing a paralytic, carried by four of them. Since they were not able to bring him to Jesus because of the crowd, they removed the roof above him, and after digging through it, they lowered the mat on which the paralytic was lying. Seeing their faith, Jesus told the paralytic, "Son, your sins are forgiven."

MARK 2:3–5

In my life there have been critical junctures where I've needed the trust of a close circle of friends. At those times I just needed people to rally around me and stand with me in prayer, in hope, and in faith. When we were getting A21 up and running, we ran into roadblock after roadblock, and I needed my circle. When my doctor called to say that I had cancer, I needed my circle. I remember a season when I felt utterly betrayed after investing deeply into a relationship, and my circle was there to help me sort through the facts and my feelings. When Mum died months too early for me, they were right there. Even when I found myself, after decades of ministry, unsure if I wanted to keep going the way I always had—all in, pressing on with the same intensity I always had—they were there to love me, pray with me, and give me their strength.

Through so many circumstances I have needed friends much like the ones depicted in Mark 2, friends who will do for us when we can't do for ourselves. Perhaps you are familiar with the story: There were four of them who carried their friend to Jesus on a stretcher. But when they got to the house where Jesus was, it was so crowded they couldn't get in. Rather than give up, they persevered, hoisting the man on the roof, cutting a hole in the roof, and then lowering him into the middle of the room, right into the presence of Jesus.[36]

Have you gathered a circle of friends who can do this kind of thing for you? Who will carry you into the presence of Jesus? We all struggle. We all fail. We all face challenges. We all face situations in which we simply do not know what to do. That's precisely why we need friends with spiritual strength. What's more, the Word goes on to say that when Jesus saw the faith of the four friends, he healed the man.[37] Did you catch that? A difference was made in the man's life all because of his friends and *their* faith, not his own.

From this story it seems there could be times when God helps us because of someone else's strength and endurance. Because of their prayers, their wisdom, their comfort, their love. There could be times when God in His great mercy uses our friends to help us keep fulfilling all that we were put on this earth to fulfill. So circle up your friends and let them carry you.

Heavenly Father, help me develop the right circle of friends, people who will be faithful and faith-filled to carry me when I can't carry myself into the presence of Jesus. In Jesus' name, amen.

73 HE WILL
STRENGTHEN YOU

"Do not fear, for I am with you; do not be afraid, for I am your God. I will strengthen you; I will help you; I will hold on to you with my righteous right hand."
ISAIAH 41:10

Around the time I turned fifty, I went to the doctor for a routine checkup. When the doctor added a test to analyze my muscle mass, I felt no concern; after all, I had been fit most of my life—or so I thought. When the test results revealed that I had 31 percent body fat, I was shocked. The healthy range for a woman my age was 21 to 25 percent. I had a hard time believing the results could be right. So I went to the gym for a second opinion. (Yes, I was in denial!)

When they tested me, they were just as quick as the doctor to inform me that I was "skinny fat." That meant I looked healthy on the outside, but inside my muscles were atrophying. I was literally losing muscle mass. I wasn't overweight, but I wasn't fit either. It was part of growing older, they said. It was then that I knew they were in a conspiracy with my doctor. What other explanation could there be?

Over time I began to accept the truth and to wrap my mind around the changes I had to make. I needed to begin lifting weights because, as I came to understand, there is no stasis mode when it comes to muscle mass. If you aren't getting stronger, you are actually getting weaker. If you aren't increasing, you are decreasing.

The first time I visited a gym, all I could do was stare at all the weights. It felt utterly overwhelming. I had no idea how to pick one up properly and not hurt myself. I had no idea how much weight was safe for me to lift. I had no idea where to begin. It was all so intimidating, but I had made the commitment to fight for my health, so I reached out to a trainer and I persevered in spite of my feelings and started building strength.

Is there something intimidating you today? Are you facing something you'd rather run and hide from than persevere through? It may be a move, a conversation, or a decision. God is with you, and He won't let go of you. He will strengthen you to keep enduring in faith.

Dare to take a step and move toward whatever it is trying to stop you. When I started lifting weights, I had no idea that hiking mountains was in my future, but God did. And He knows what's in your future too. Let Him strengthen you.

Heavenly Father, please help me not be afraid and intimidated, but to put my trust in You, remembering that You are with me and You will strengthen me. In Jesus' name, amen.

74 CHOOSE THE ONE WHO CHOOSES US

We don't dare classify or compare ourselves with some who commend themselves. But in measuring themselves by themselves and comparing themselves to themselves, they lack understanding.

2 CORINTHIANS 10:12

I 'll never forget the sinking feeling I often had when I was young and my classmates were picking teams for netball—a game similar to basketball, only once you have the ball in your hands you have to be still until you pass it on. Two girls were the captains, and they would take turns picking from the crowd to form the two teams. If you were last, one captain would turn to the other and say, "You can have them." I remember the anxiety of standing there hoping I wouldn't be last. It was such a terrible feeling. To this day, I can't stand to watch TV shows where one is chosen and one is rejected. It makes me feel just like I did waiting to be chosen all over again. Why is it that in our world it seems like the ones we choose and celebrate are the best looking, most gifted, most talented, most charismatic—and the rest go unseen? I'm glad it's not that way to God; no one is unseen to God. He chooses us all.

Still, when I was in school, I had none of that understanding, and I walked away from netball-team-picking with a terrible sense of comparison. Whether it was in netball, some other sport, or academics, I learned this practice of measuring. Of comparing myself to all the others and figuring out where I fell in the order of things. It turned into a miserable cycle, because one week I might think I was somewhere near the top of the list—for any number of reasons—and the next week I felt like I had fallen to the bottom of the list.

If only all this comparison we learned stopped when we left school, but you and I both know it doesn't. To this day I feel sure we all know what it's like to have comparison shrink us, paralyze us, or cripple us emotionally. What if we make a concentrated effort starting today to minimize comparison in our lives everywhere we can? We could start in our social media worlds, perhaps by stepping back from scrolling through everyone's lives and comparing theirs to ours. I understand that it can be a hard thing to walk away from, especially if our phones are connected to our work and daily schedules, but I have found that if we are constantly scrolling and comparing, we are most likely not pressing for the prize that is ours in Christ Jesus. In fact, if we are spending our time trying to figure out how to make our lives look like someone else's, we are not moving forward. If we are feeling defeated and deflated, we are not persevering. And if we are not persevering, most likely we're being drawn off course, away from our calling, away from enduring in our faith. And none of us wants that, do we?

Let's redirect our focus today. Let's walk away from comparison in every way we can and press on for more of Jesus. Let's choose the One who always chooses us.

Jesus, please help me stop looking around at everyone else running their race and comparing my race to theirs. Please help me reset my focus on running my own. In Your name, amen.

75 HIS PERFECT PACE

Ahimaaz son of Zadok said, "Please let me run and tell the king the good news that the LORD has vindicated him by freeing him from his enemies."

Joab replied to him, "You are not the man to take good news today. You may do it another day, but today you aren't taking good news, because the king's son is dead."

2 SAMUEL 18:19–20

Running has been a part of my life since I was in my early twenties, and for years it was the primary way I exercised. Nowadays I mix it up with weightlifting, hiking, boxing, and any new sport that builds more endurance and strength. But, no doubt, a good run of five to seven miles on a beach somewhere still gives me such satisfaction. Maybe that's why I can relate so personally to our walk with Christ being a race we're to run. With endurance. Lasting the distance. Running hard at times and pausing to rest and replenish other times. In fact, my knees talk back to me more these days, so I have to recognize when it's a good day to run and perhaps when I should work out in the gym.

You could say I have come to value the importance of timing, both physically and spiritually. Just as there are times to go for a good run on the beach and times not to, there are definite seasons to be sensitive to in our spiritual race, and it's important to learn how to discern the season we're in—and what our response should be in that particular season. If we don't discern our own race and its timing accurately, we're more likely to experience the kinds of things we don't want. Things like disappointment, frustration, failure, or confusion.

I realize that today's verse may not be on your next top ten to memorize, but it shows us the importance of timing. After winning a battle, Ahimaaz wanted to run and tell King David the good news. But Joab knew what Ahimaaz didn't, so he basically said, "The timing is not yet right; you can't take the news today; you may do it another day." Isn't that what God wants us to understand sometimes? Not today, but maybe later?

Think of it this way. Have you ever felt you were ready for a promotion, but your leader said it wasn't time? I know there have been plenty of times in my life when I thought I was ready, but the leader above me didn't see it that way. Or have you ever wanted to run ahead of God and do something you weren't yet called to do and get to where you were not yet meant to be? When I have made such mistakes, I have felt so upset with myself, but each time God in His great mercy has always helped me persevere and find the way forward, all the while growing in my discernment of His timing.

Let's keep working at this together. Let's go to God and ask Him to help us be even more sensitive to His timing. That way we can keep running our race in step with His perfect pace.

Heavenly Father, please help me grow in my discernment of Your timing. Help me be more sensitive to Your Holy Spirit and Your leading. In Jesus' name, amen.

PART 4

PATIENCE: OUR STRENGTH IN THE WAITING

Climb the mountain not to plant your flag, but to embrace the challenge, enjoy the air and behold the view. Climb it so you can see the world, not so the world can see you.

DAVID MCCULLOUGH JR.

76 WATCH THE COOKIES BAKE

But the fruit of the Spirit is . . . patience.

GALATIANS 5:22

Patience is my least favorite word in the English language. If you were to ask anyone in my family or someone who works with me, most likely they would acknowledge that while I have gifts and have worked hard to develop the fruit of the Spirit, patience is the one thing that still feels like it's in embryonic form. I feel sure somewhere in my spirit this seed is just waiting to sprout, but I know from the times when my patience has been tested that it has yet to come into full bloom.

It's not because I haven't fertilized it and watered it faithfully, because I have. For years. With the Word and in everyday situations I face. When I'm stuck in traffic. When I'm waiting because my flight has been delayed—again. When I'm waiting in the car in the driveway for the girls to come get in. We've all been there, right? Still, it remains a struggle. Even when I do something as basic as baking cookies, my lack of patience can get the best of me—and the cookies.

To this day, when my girls smell cookies baking, they come rushing to the kitchen because they know I'm going to do one of two things. I'm either going to pull them out too soon because I've got things to do and I can't stand waiting one more minute on them, or I'm going to wander off and start doing something else I need to do and completely forget about them. So I specialize in either cookies that are the equivalent of warm dough or ones that are more than well done, perhaps with some burned edges as a bonus. Suffice it to say, it's best that I leave the cookie-baking to Catherine and Sophia. I have good intentions but not enough patience.

What about you? What are the things that try your patience? What stretches you to grow more of this fruit of the Spirit in your life? I'll admit that my first thought every time my patience is tried is not to grow and develop more fruit, but overall I have grown significantly through the years of my life. And I have used many a trying moment as an opportunity to change. I'm so grateful that God is patient, and He is patient with me as I keep working on this.

He's patient with you too. As you move through your day and things start to try your patience, recognize it as an opportunity to develop more of the fruit God wants to grow in you. Recognize it as another way you build endurance so you can keep moving forward full of vitality and strength, fulfilling all that God's called you to do. Even if it's something as simple as watching the cookies bake until they are just right.

Heavenly Father, please help me in the everyday moments when my patience is tried. Help me recognize the opportunity before me to develop more of this fruit of the Spirit. In Jesus' name, amen.

77 THE WAY HE PROMISED

Rejoice in hope; be patient in affliction; be persistent in prayer.
ROMANS 12:12

I have a dear friend who has endured more in her life than my heart and mind can comprehend, but to sit with her and listen to her faith and resilience is beyond inspiring. In fact, I always look forward to meeting up with her when I speak near her hometown.

When we first met, I would have never guessed the heartache she had lived through. I was hosting an A21 awareness trip in Thessaloniki, Greece, for a group of women from her church. Over a lunch of Greek salad with extra feta cheese, we clicked. She is Lebanese and Syrian, and with me being Greek, we joked that maybe it was because of our Mediterranean blood. It was fun to meet a woman who could talk as fast as me; was as passionate, driven, and focused as me; and gestured with her hands as much as I did. One evening, at a tiny Greek restaurant, our dinner transitioned into a late-night conversation about everything, including all the loss she had endured and the despair she had felt.

There was such pain in her eyes as she told me of her multiple miscarriages and about finally accepting that the baby she had wanted most in her life could never be delivered into her arms. I recognized in her the same agonized look I had seen before in the eyes of so many women—women who were desperate to have a child, who tried every possible procedure to become pregnant. I couldn't imagine the hopelessness she had known, living through such a cycle of suffering and spending more than a decade desperately trying to carry a child to term. But here she was, somehow having found a way to trust God again after all her hope had been lost. I was captivated by her faith, and I wanted to know more.

When she went on to tell me more of her story, with chapters of betrayal, divorce, health issues, and the loss of friends and loved ones at critical junctures of her life, I sat there stunned. How could someone walk through so much and still be full of hope and enduring faith?

What especially got my attention is how she began her story—and then how she ended it. She told me that when she was just a girl, God put it in her heart to be a mother to the nations. That promise was the hope she held on to all the years she longed to have her own child. By the time we met, she had served on a board for an organization that served to protect women and children. After so many years and trials, she had become a mother to nations, just as God had promised. All I could do was marvel at the goodness of God, the faithfulness of God, and the enduring hope of my new friend.

What is it that you have longed so desperately for? Rejoice in hope. Be patient in affliction and persistent in prayer. And watch God unfold your future the way He promised.

Heavenly Father, please help me be patient in affliction, trusting You, enduring in faith, letting You unfold my purpose and Your plans for my life. In Jesus' name, amen.

78 LET PATIENCE WORK

Let patience have its perfect work, that you may be perfect and complete, lacking nothing.

JAMES 1:4 NKJV

When our girls were young, Nick and I took them to an amusement park for a day of fun. Because the park was crowded and the lines were long at each ride, there were signs letting everyone know how long to expect to wait before boarding a ride. When we got in a line warning us it would be sixty minutes, Nick wasn't sure if it was a good idea—not because of the heat or because our girls wouldn't last that long, but because of me. I'm not exactly known as the most patient member of our family. But on that particular day, I was determined to grow in patience and let God build endurance in my heart, so I convinced him that I was up for the challenge. I wish I could tell you how I passed the test that day with flying colors and Nick and the girls all gave glory to God, but that wouldn't be an accurate account. Suffice it to say, my patience project was an epic fail, and Nick and the girls continue to tell the story about how many times I complained in those sixty minutes.

The good news is I don't give up easily. To this day I'm still growing in patience, and because I'm so aware that it doesn't come naturally to me, I often say today's verse to myself and to God in prayer. I want patience and the promise that comes with it. I know that to fulfill all that God's called me to do, to become all that He wants me to be, there are things I can't lack. I need Jesus to fill all the gaps in my life and work—between what I have and don't have, between what I need and have yet to receive, between where I've been developed spiritually and where I have yet to develop. And apparently if I let patience have its perfect work, eventually I'll lack nothing.

So every time I feel impatience creeping in, I say this verse to myself. Sometimes we all need to have a good conversation with ourselves, don't we? I often look in the mirror and start talking: "Christine, let patience work in you. You can't fast-track it. God is preparing you for what He's prepared for you, and He wants you to lack no good thing. The only way you are going to become more Christlike is if you let patience have its perfect work in you." I'll talk that way as long as it takes for my inner self to calm down and transition into practicing patience.

Maybe patience is easy for you, or maybe you're like me and it's something you have to work on almost continually. The good news is if you keep working on it, you will grow. I've come a long way since that day we were waiting in an unending line to ride a sixty-second ride. Let's be committed together to letting patience have its perfect work in us.

Heavenly Father, thank You for letting the sprout of patience fully bloom in my life. Help me mature and develop further in this area. In Jesus' name, amen.

79 A NEW SEASON

There is an occasion for everything, and a time for every activity under heaven.

ECCLESIASTES 3:1

Though I love to cook, there have been seasons of my life when I've rarely had time for it. In fact, in 2020, when we were locked down for so long due to the pandemic, it had been so long since I'd cooked regularly that I think my daughters were genuinely surprised at my cooking skills. I suppose they had come to think all I knew how to do was make reservations. One time Catherine's teacher asked her students what their mother's favorite thing to make was, and Catherine proudly said, "Reservations!"

As mothers, it's hard not to wonder what our children's teachers think of us since we have no idea what our kids say about us all day for months of the year! I've learned to go to those parent-teacher nights with my head held high and acting like everything in the Caine household is completely normal, whatever normal is. Because let's face it: we're all called to forge our own lives the way God directs us, and normal for me might look completely different from what normal is for you. What matters most is that we're pursuing God as we're building our homes, and that may look different from one home to the next.

But in full disclosure, in the season when Catherine gave everyone at school a glimpse into our home life, we were traveling quite a bit, and reservations had become my go-to. It was either that or we ordered takeout and brought it home. And at some restaurants we frequented, we were on a first-name basis with the waitstaff. Maybe you've been there when your kids' football, baseball, or soccer season was in full swing, or when you had to travel every week for work or school or medical treatments. Sometimes the season we're in can control our schedule, and as much as we'd like to go at a slower pace, we can't. There are things to be done for one reason or another.

When I've been in those spans of time, I've had to remind myself to be patient with the season, to recognize that it won't last forever, and to make the best of it. I've known parents who turned late nights into pizza parties, out-of-town trips into pajama parties, and endless hours at ball fields into family picnics.

The times when we've had to eat out more than I might have preferred, I've had to quit stressing about how many vegetables my girls were eating, or how late we would be up, or if we would ever get to eat consistently around our own dinner table again. I had to remind myself to be patient in the season in which we were living.

What season are you in? Is it one where you can't control everything you'd like? Use it as an opportunity to exercise patience and build endurance internally. After all, before you know it, a new season will come.

Heavenly Father, please help me recognize that life is full of seasons, and teach me how to be patient in the one I am in. In Jesus' name, amen.

80 FAITH AND PATIENCE

We desire each of you to demonstrate the same diligence for the full assurance of your hope until the end, so that you won't become lazy but will be imitators of those who inherit the promises through faith and perseverance [patience].

HEBREWS 6:11–12

can't count the times I've had to remind myself of this verse, because it is through faith *and* patience we inherit the promises of God. Not one or the other. They work in tandem. Personally I love the faith part because I don't struggle with that as much. Throwing a faith challenge in front of me gets my spiritual adrenaline pumping. If you want me to climb a mountain, literally or spiritually, then game on. But when you remind me of the patience part, it somewhat dampens my enthusiasm because being patient is not my natural inclination.

When I'm around people who are patient, I marvel at them. Their temperament seems so calm. They seem to naturally be good with how long anything and everything takes. If only that were me. Whether it's the checkout line at the store, the security line at an airport, or waiting on the promises of God, I'd rather we speed things along, and preferably at my pace.

Still, I have learned that if we will exercise patience and keep enduring in faith for as long as it takes, the promise will come. The dreams, goals, and plans God has placed in our hearts take time—most often, lots of time. There are some things God put in my heart more than two decades ago that I'm just now seeing happen. It's taken that long, but I never let go of doing my best to walk in faith *and* patience.

What has God placed in your heart? Maybe you've wanted to start a business, go back to school, volunteer in your community, adopt a child, or go on a mission trip. Maybe you've been praying for years for someone to follow Christ or draw closer to Him. Whatever it is, keep exercising faith *and* patience. From all I've learned, *faith* is believing God, believing that He is who He says He is and that He will do what He said He would do. *Patience* is our capacity to tolerate delay—to wait. It's trusting that God is good, God does good, and God knows what He is doing—no matter how long it takes and no matter what our purpose may be.

I understand that walking in faith and patience often feels counter-cultural. We live in a world connected globally by the internet and social media, so we have instant access to everything from news to products to real-time videos of world events. We consider it normal to access everything instantly. But in our lives, there might be years of hard work in between the beginning of something and when we see it come to pass. There are significant life lessons to be learned in the years of working toward a goal. There are experiences God wants us to go through that take time so He can prepare us for the future He's designed for us. And all of it requires we walk in both faith *and* patience so we can inherit everything God has for us.

Heavenly Father, I embrace enduring in faith and exercising patience for all that You've promised me. I trust You and Your timing for everything in my life. In Jesus' name, amen.

81 THE FINISH LINE

The end of a matter is better than its beginning; a patient spirit is better than a proud spirit.

ECCLESIASTES 7:8

As I approached the last two weeks of earning my master's in leadership and evangelism from Wheaton College, I couldn't believe what I had accomplished. And I couldn't help but remember how intimidated I felt when I first started. I was plagued with the idea of wondering if I'd fail. After all, it had been more than thirty years since I'd been in school. It was like the anxiety of kindergarten came over me and flooded my thoughts. What if I got in trouble for talking? Do they get onto you for such things in college? It was hilarious what all went through my mind.

But here I was nearing the finish line. It had been four years of working on what's normally a two-year degree, because I did it through the very first Propel Cohort—a program we coordinated with Wheaton. Along with twenty other Propel women, we met for a week at a time, two times a year, and attended lectures and completed all our research, assignments, and papers in between. Working all this in while being married, being a mother, working, traveling, and speaking was so different from when I went to Sydney University for my bachelor's. Back then I was in my early twenties, single, living at home, and had very few responsibilities.

All I can say is that King Solomon knew what he was talking about when he said the end of a matter is better than its beginning. When we finish something, especially something that takes years to accomplish, it works so much into us, something far more than knowledge. It works into us things like confidence, understanding, and revelation. It even builds in us more patience and endurance.

There are so many things in this life you can't rush. Like school. Whether you are in elementary school, high school, college, or any other coursework, we all know that you have to successfully do the work in one level to move to the next level. My courses were often tagged with 101, 201, 301, and finally, 401! I couldn't take 401 until I had taken all the others in sequential order. The educational system sets the pace, and as much as we might want to rush it, very few of us get to skip a class or skip a grade. We don't get to go from start to finish in a single bound.

Are you moving through something methodical? Something that requires a steady, forced pace and that cannot be rushed? Rest in that pace. Settle into the rhythm. Let God use it to build patience and endurance in you. Then, when you get to the finish line, dance all the way across it and celebrate what hard work and a patient spirit did for you!

Heavenly Father, please help me appreciate the endurance and patience You are building in me with every deliberate, methodical step in my life. In Jesus' name, amen.

82 THE LONG WAY AROUND

When Pharaoh let the people go, God did not lead them on the road through the Philistine country, though that was shorter. For God said, "If they face war, they might change their minds and return to Egypt." So God led the people around by the desert road toward the Red Sea.
EXODUS 13:17–18 NIV

When we travel, Nick is the navigator. Using apps, he figures out exactly where we need to go. I always feel so relaxed because the app shows all these little red lines where the traffic is heavy and suggests alternate routes to get around traffic jams. What I especially appreciate is it can even direct us to the nearest coffee shop—something invaluable to my earthly existence.

But sometimes Nick likes to take shortcuts. While that sounds good, it's not—because his shortcuts aren't always shorter. Still, he insists they are the way to go. Though they try my patience quite a bit, I've resigned myself to the fact that there's no talking him out of it. The best thing I can do is congratulate him when they do work and not utter a word when they don't. After all these years of watching Nick navigate cities around the world—and take many lengthy shortcuts—I've derived some well-thought-out spiritual principles based on our experiences with (and without) an app. Mostly because I've had a lot of time to think while riding in the car during all those shortcuts.

Like the apps, God knows the traffic jams ahead. He knows the road closures and the accidents blocking the way. So He reroutes us the way He knows is best for us instead of letting us take a misguided shortcut. Isn't that what He did for the children of Israel? Rather than lead them on an established trade route—that was hundreds of miles shorter than the one they took around to the Red Sea—God led the children of Israel on the long desert road. Why? Because God knew best. He knew the Philistines were an aggressive people and that if the Israelites were attacked, they might turn back. They weren't trained to be warriors. So He took them the long way around.

The same principle applies to us. Even when there is a tempting shortcut, God knows what's best. He uses the long way around to protect us and to prepare us, to build endurance in us. Sometimes our long road takes the form of anonymity, obscurity, long hours, or uncomfortable conditions. Sometimes it can leave us thinking, *I've missed it* or *God has forgotten me.* Sometimes it can leave us waiting so long we feel worn down and our hopes are dimmed.

Still, He is with us. He won't leave us. He can't forget us. So let's keep moving forward, exercising patience, and trusting Him as we travel the long way around.

Heavenly Father, please help me trust You more, no matter how long the road seems. Help me resist the shortcuts that are certain to lead where I don't really want to go, and guide me to be patient in my walk with You. In Jesus' name, amen.

83 BE PATIENT WITH
YOUR HEALING

Love is patient, love is kind.

1 CORINTHIANS 13:4

A ll throughout my life, when I've encountered a situation where I wasn't sure what to do, God has always been faithful to bring someone along to guide me in the right direction. To help me keep enduring in faith. Such was the case when my mum passed away and it triggered a season of grieving not only her loss but also the loss of never getting to know my biological mother. It was a time when I had more questions than answers and absolutely no idea how to solve the riddles in my heart.

It was during that time that we had a family over for dinner, and during conversation, they shared how their adopted son went through a period of questioning and searching and that a counselor who specialized in family-of-origin issues had helped tremendously. Never had I heard of such a person—a Christian family-of-origin counselor? What did that mean? Our friends explained that the counselor had more than twenty years of experience helping people piece together clues from the past to better understand the present. My friends had no idea what I had been going through, but God knew, and He was at it again, leading me to someone who could help me. And, as always, His timing was perfect—the right person at the right time with the right connection to the next step.

Listening to our friends share what a help this counselor had been to their family, I felt a sense of release to go in search of more details. Though I knew various facts about my birth mother's life, it seemed that it was time to dig a little further into *who* she was—and perhaps how that had affected who I had become.

I met with the counselor for several sessions, and of all the insights I gained, the most profound was when she said, "Christine, do you realize that your biological mother was quite probably exploited by your father, and here you are rescuing women around the world from being exploited as well?" I was stunned. Never had I considered such a thought. What I could only see as painful, I could now see as part of my purpose. I could see how God was once more taking the broken pieces of my life and using them for His good and His glory. He had rescued me to help rescue others.

If you've invited Him in to begin a healing work in you, resist the urge to rush it. Resist the desire to get it over with as quickly as possible. I know how painful it can be. But be patient with yourself, and with God and His timing. That's what doing the hard work of becoming whole can feel like, but it is totally worth it. Yield to God's healing work in your heart and His perfect pace. Trust Him that He knows how much you can take in this season and in the next, and in all the seasons to come. Remember, His love is patient and kind forevermore.

Heavenly Father, please help me rest in Your timing, particularly when it comes to the healing of my heart and all the hidden places that haven't been exposed. In Jesus' name, amen.

84 WAITING WELL

Wait for the LORD; be strong, and let your heart be courageous. Wait for the LORD.

PSALM 27:14

___

am as enthusiastic about waiting as I am for getting a cavity filled. In case you can't tell, I absolutely have an aversion to waiting. There have been times when I wanted a hot coffee badly—when I needed a hot coffee badly—but because I can't bear the thought of waiting, I've settled for an iced coffee because it's faster. Such a move sounds harmless, I know, but it exposes the truth. Of all my strengths, of all the attributes every personality test has ever exposed, patience—something necessary for waiting—has never come out on top. And yet it seems to be important to God that I understand the importance of waiting and knowing how to wait well. So, while I may find a way to get out of waiting for my coffee, there are plenty of opportunities to wait that I'll never find a way around. God wants me to practice waiting and learning how to wait His way.

Part of how we're to wait can be found in today's verse. According to this scripture, we're to be strong and let our heart be courageous *while* we wait for God. This tells me that waiting is not a place of passivity but a place of pursuit. It's a posture. An action. One definition I've read says it's "to stay in a place of expectation."[38]

Sometimes when I've been in a season of waiting, I have felt held in position, and the only way I can manage the tension of that feeling is to make sure I'm waiting the way God wants—with expectancy, looking forward, moving forward, taking the next right step, daring to keep my hopes up even when everything looks hopeless. It's never easy, but when I wait God's way, when I trust in spite of what I can't see, I can almost feel the endurance being built inside me. It's like a painful, stretching sensation in my heart, in the place that's doing its best to be courageous when everything in my mind wants to fold.

Have you ever evaluated the way you wait? Are you patient? Are you mentally, emotionally, and spiritually in a place of pursuit? God is always pursuing us, right? He never stops, so neither should we stop pursuing Him. He isn't dormant in our waiting season, so we probably shouldn't be dormant in it either. God is always working in our waiting seasons, so let's be working too. Let's be working with the sense that we're waiting with expectation. Looking beyond our moment of containment and confinement to when we see what we are hoping and praying to see.

Father, please help me grow in patience, learning how to wait well on Your timing. Help me stay in a place of pursuit, looking forward and taking the next right step. In Jesus' name, amen.

85 LET'S GROW AGELESS

He has made everything appropriate in its time. He has also put eternity in their hearts, but no one can discover the work God has done from beginning to end.

ECCLESIASTES 3:11

God's will is that we live—really live—maximizing every moment of every day. I suppose, in this season of my life, climbing mountains is part of that for me. I want to do something new. I want to see something new. I want to feel something new. I want to feel alive. I imagine this is how we all feel; otherwise, apart from difficult or unusual circumstances, we wouldn't work so hard to stay alive, would we?

At the same time, I find that while we're doing our best to live life to the fullest, we also want to look untouched by age. I'm not sure how you make it to one hundred without a single wrinkle, but just think of all the creams, potions, and serums we've purchased in hopes of hanging on to younger-looking skin. Think of all the times we've updated our clothes, our hair, or our makeup to somehow roll back the clock. Sometimes my girls try to break it to me gently that I am out of style or that my shoes are so last year. "Mum," they'll say, "I think you can do better." I can't help but laugh, because invariably it will be about my favorite shirt or sneakers, the ones that I've gotten all broken in, perfectly stained and stretched out of shape.

I don't like being the one to break it to us all, but no matter what we do, we will age. God set it up that way. But rather than getting caught up focusing on the external, what God really wants us to focus on is the internal. That's where we'll find the true source for living ageless—full of passion and zeal, full of Him and who He is, full of enduring in faith and fulfilling all the purpose He placed in our hearts. After all, God placed the desire for eternity in our hearts so we would pursue it and discover our life in Him. So we would learn how to really live.

When I look back on my life, I can see how God was always trying to get me to see this, long before I was old enough to even care about wrinkles. The first time I began to hear of His salvation, I was about fourteen. The next time was in high school. By the time I was twenty-one, my heart was more than ready. The longing for eternity He placed in my heart came into full bloom, and I couldn't help but reach for Him and give myself to Him fully.

I'm so thankful that God patiently awakened the desire for eternity He placed in my heart. That He patiently wooed my focus from the external to the internal. One moment at a time. Can you look back and see how He orchestrated your path to becoming a devoted follower of Jesus? Can you see how He patiently led you toward Him one step at a time?

Let's remember this when we pray for people, as we continue to endure in faith for them, hoping and believing that they will become followers of Jesus. After all, God has placed eternity in their hearts, just like He did ours.

Father, please help me be as patient as You as I continue to pray for my friends and loved ones to become fully devoted followers of Jesus. It's only a matter of time. In Jesus' name, amen.

86 AN ON-TIME GOD

From ancient times no one has heard, no one has listened to, no eye has seen any God except you who acts on behalf of the one who waits for him.
ISAIAH 64:4

We live in a world that has conditioned us to expect instant results. In most places, we have grown to enjoy overnight delivery of almost everything, if not same-day delivery. We can have groceries, a mattress, a book, or an appliance delivered right to our doorstep within twenty-four hours. We can even get a ride within minutes with an app. And if we're hungry, we can schedule a reservation time online so we don't have to show up and wait in line at a restaurant, or we can order food picked up and delivered to our door. From my perspective, it's as though our convenient and fast-tracked world is robbing us of the opportunity to develop patience. I can hear you cheering now, because who wants to develop patience?

None of us, I know. But we need it, don't we? Especially when it comes to waiting on God to answer our prayers, to help us fulfill our purpose or carry out His plans for our lives. Isn't that what Isaiah wrote? It's when we wait on God that we see Him act on our behalf.

Still, I know it's not easy to wait. It's hard enough to wait for any reason, much less to wait on God for whatever it is we've taken to Him in prayer—especially when it's something He's placed in our hearts in the first place.

It's an interesting journey to know the very thing God wants us to do but not be able to get it done quickly. But that's how it often works, doesn't it? More than thirty years ago, God placed desires in my heart, things big and small, but He knew all along that none of them would come to pass for decades. He needed to prepare me for the very things He was preparing for me. I wasn't ready before I was ready, even though I am sure I would have thought I was ready. I had to learn to pray for things and then trust God for His timing.

Isn't that what we often remind one another? God's timing is perfect. I've said it plenty of times, and I believe it's true, especially the longer I walk with Him. While I haven't always understood why God delayed something, sometimes for years, once it came to pass I could see why people or circumstances had to fall into place first. Walking long enough with Him to see this process unfold encourages me that He truly is an on-time God and that waiting for something from Him is always worth it.

Are you waiting for something right now? Have you been waiting for a really long time? As hard as it is, I have found that if we're willing to wait and trust, we will see our lives become so much more effective and so much more fruitful. He truly is an on-time God.

Heavenly Father, please help me rest and trust in Your timing. Help me remember that You really are an on-time God. In Jesus' name, amen.

87 PATIENCE EQUALS ENDURANCE

Since the day we heard this, we haven't stopped praying for you . . . so that you may have great endurance and patience.

COLOSSIANS 1:9, 11

A s a youth leader in my early twenties, I spent many hours driving to country towns in Australia to help encourage youth leaders and speak in schools and at evangelistic events. I was passionate and committed, often driving up to eight hours at a time to reach underserviced areas. I loved seeing young people place their hope in Jesus, and I loved building youth ministries, but there were times when I felt extremely lonely.

In those days, there was no such thing as cell phones to call your friends and connect. There were no podcasts or satellite radio shows to listen away the miles. All I had was a limited number of sermons on cassette that I spent hours listening to, praying, and doing my best to keep my mind on what mattered most. Given the circumstances, it was easy to feel isolated and lonely.

It didn't help that although I was seeing great fruit, my family was not supportive of my choice to leave the corporate world to step into ministry, many of my friends were getting married and starting families, and others were thriving in their careers. They thought I was crazy to leave everything behind in order to reach young people with the gospel. Without family and friends to encourage and support me, in my aloneness, I would sometimes find myself attending my own pity party and imagine what my life may have looked like had I continued with my career path.

It was during those long drives that I was learning to be content in Christ, that my motives were being purified, that my commitment was being strengthened, that I was learning endurance and patience as the miles slipped by. I find it no coincidence that the Greek root word for patience is *hupomoné*, which is the exact same Greek root word for endurance.[39] Just like endurance, being patient is the act of remaining under pressure when we'd rather hit the escape valve. Had it not been for the conviction in my heart that I was where God wanted me to be, I might have given in to the pressure of loneliness. Maybe you're under such pressure now. Maybe you're staying in a job you'd rather leave. Maybe you're staying in a volunteer position you'd rather hand off. Maybe you're keeping a commitment you'd rather renege on.

I understand there are times to leave something, but when we know it's a place God wants us, we have to exercise patience and stay steady. Is there an area of your life where you need to apply patience? Settle in your heart today that rather than hit the escape valve, you'll stay on mission by staying put.

Heavenly Father, please give me the strength to continue walking in patience, staying obedient by staying put. Help me choose to keep building endurance. In Jesus' name, amen.

88 GOD IS PATIENT, ALWAYS

Therefore the LORD is waiting to show you mercy, and is rising up to show you compassion, for the LORD is a just God. All who wait patiently for him are happy.
ISAIAH 30:18

B eing in ministry for almost all my adult life has taught me to be patient with my brothers and sisters in Christ. Being married for more than twenty-five years has taught me to be patient with my husband. Being a mother for twenty years has taught me to be patient with my children. Being a Christ-follower who prays has taught me to wait patiently on God. Now, I don't always get it right, but overall, I have grown in patience because of prayers, relationships, and positions that required patience. At the same time, I feel sure I have given many people the opportunity to practice patience with me, whether they asked for it or not. No doubt, God has a sense of humor. It seems there's no other way to grow patience than to practice patience, something that builds endurance in us.

But the person I have always found most challenging to be patient with is me. To give myself grace, to give myself space, to forgive myself, and to say to myself all the things I would say to my husband, one of my daughters, or a discouraged friend—that is something I work on to this day. It feels far more natural to critique how I could have said something better or handled a situation with more finesse. It has taken me years of renewing my mind to train myself not to ruminate over what I cannot change, to give it to God and to trust Him.

What about you? Do you find it easier to be more patient with others than with yourself? Think about the last time you made a mistake. Did your first thoughts include giving yourself grace like this: *It's okay; your heart was in the right place; you did your best; you can try again tomorrow?* Or was it more like negative self-talk and flustered emotions?

I understand we live in a world that constantly reminds us how we're not enough. We feel unrelenting pressure to do more, be more, or get more. At home. At work. Even in places as routine as the checkout line at the grocery store there are racks of magazines telling us we're not thin enough, beautiful enough, athletic enough, maternal enough, sexy enough. It's exhausting. On social media, all we need to do is scroll for sixty seconds and we'll see what we're missing, what we're not enough of, and where we haven't been.

Maybe that means it's time to put down our phones more and start exercising patience toward ourselves. Maybe it's time to take our focus off how we think we might not measure up and turn our hearts and minds toward the One who is more than enough—toward God Himself. Doesn't that take the pressure off? Doesn't that shift our perspective? I think so. Then, out of that place of being patient with ourselves, of being gracious with ourselves and looking to Him, we can begin to see ourselves more the way He does—as someone who is waiting to show us mercy, who is rising up to show us compassion. Always.

Father, thank You for always being eager to show me mercy, to be gracious to me, and show me compassion. Help me be patient with myself the way You are. In Jesus' name, amen.

89 HAVE PATIENCE IN THE PRUNING

Every branch in me that does not produce fruit he removes, and he prunes every branch that produces fruit so that it will produce more fruit.
JOHN 15:2

I had always dreamed of helping to build a life-giving, gospel-centered church in Greece. As we all know, I love all things Greek, I am Greek, and the Bible is full of amazing things God has done in Greece, so I wanted to see God do the same kind of marvelous works in Greece in our day—especially among the young people. In 2012, this dream came true when we planted Zoe Church in Thessaloniki, the same city where Paul preached a few months before he wrote the letters to the Thessalonians.

It was an exciting and daunting time for our team. They worked night and day to get the church off the ground; they wanted to see the people in Thessaloniki discover the hope and faith that can only be found in Jesus. But like most every assignment from God, there were setbacks, unexpected roadblocks, and disappointments. More than once it would have been easier to give up and disband. To give in to all the pressure of trying to do a work that felt impossible. But we knew God had led us to start the church, so we kept moving forward.

The first three years, I wondered if anything was happening. The team kept showing up, praying, serving, and believing. They were faithful and patient. But looking at the bigger picture, I often felt discouraged.

We were constantly evaluating our outreaches and programs and whether we should alter them in some way. At times, what we thought was flourishing, God seemed to be pruning. In one season people began leaving and it looked like the doors were starting to close, something we never imagined at the onset. But then people started bringing their friends, and we began to catch glimpses of people's lives being changed.

Looking back on those early years of the church, I have discovered that God prunes not only what's not bearing fruit but also what is bearing fruit—all because He wants to see everything bear even more fruit. In fact, the Word tells us He wants to see us bear much fruit, and fruit that will remain.[40] That's what He's after. And that's why pruning is so important. Today, Zoe is a healthy, growing church.

Are you in a pruning season? Do you feel like God is pruning what's not fruitful or what is fruitful? Remember, He prunes both. If you're in a pruning season, be patient with the pruning process. Be patient with God and trust that He wants to see you flourish in every area of your life. I understand that if you're like me, you'll just want to get it over with. Pruning rarely feels comfortable because it literally means to cut off or to eliminate superfluous matter.[41] But I have found that God is a loving and meticulous Gardener. He knows exactly what He's doing. Let Him cut away what needs to go so something else can grow. Let the Master Gardener do His work so you can truly flourish.

Heavenly Father, help me trust in Your loving and meticulous gardening skills. Help me exercise patience while You prune me so I will flourish. In Jesus' name, amen.

90 PATIENCE BY
ENDURING

Being strengthened with all power, according to his glorious might, so that
you may have great endurance and patience, joyfully giving thanks to the
Father, who has enabled you to share in the saints' inheritance in the light.
COLOSSIANS 1:11–12

Mount Whitney, in California's southern Sierra, is the highest peak in the lower forty-eight states of the US. To get to the top of the 14,000-plus-foot peak requires a permit. The good news is the Inyo National Forest holds a lottery every year to award permits so hikers can plan their summit day.[42] And despite the fact that only about 30 percent of those who participate in the lottery win, Dawn did. In fact, she got permits for four of us to make the climb together.

At first it felt surreal to me. I was so excited. We were going to get to climb one of the highest mountains in the country. Then it hit me. Though I had enjoyed recreational hiking for years, I had only begun seriously climbing mountains a little more than a year before. The longest I had hiked was eight hours. This was going to be a seventeen-hour hike. I started researching hiking all over again. I watched videos of the trek up Mount Whitney. I read more on managing the elevation gain and adjusting to altitude changes. It wasn't Mount Everest, of course, but to me it might as well have been.

There was no question that I had to begin training right away. From the time we won our permits to the climb would be a short three months. My first weekend out I started with walking up and down steep hills for two hours straight. It was grueling, and I longed for an easier way to get fit to climb Mt. Whitney, but there was no other way. My second weekend out, Dawn led our tribe of four up above the clouds to the top of Mount Baden-Powell, one of eight peaks we planned to hike in preparation.

What I experienced is what I've learned over and over throughout my life. There is no way to bypass the process of building endurance. Not physically and not spiritually. In our internal lives, to build endurance, to build spiritual muscle, we must go through the painful process of building it. And the process of building anything requires patience. As much as I would have loved to train quickly, there was no way to do that. All I could do was go out weekend after weekend and put one foot in front of the other and work out during the week at home. It was a slow and tedious journey.

Paul wrote to the Colossians that he and Timothy prayed for them that they would be strengthened with all power, that they would have great endurance and patience. I have found that we can't have one without the other. To endure requires patience, and patience is built by enduring, so let's keep doing both!

Heavenly Father, please help me exercise patience while I build endurance, and endure while I build patience! I see how I can't have one without the other. In Jesus' name, amen.

91 CLOUDY JUDGMENT

The first to state his case seems right until another comes and cross-examines him.

PROVERBS 18:17

When my girls were younger, like most siblings, they could get into spats over the smallest thing, usually when they were tired and needed a nap. Sometimes it was a disagreement over which video to watch, or who got on the couch first, or what snack to eat. Honestly, it could be about anything. With Catherine being four years older than Sophia, she was often the more patient one and the one who gave in more. Watching her, I always appreciated the love and consideration she extended. I'm not so sure I was that forgiving toward my brothers. I remember us being more the type who fought it out until someone won—unless, of course, my mother intervened. Maybe having brothers made me tougher in ways neither of my girls have ever had to be. Who knows?

But when my girls couldn't find an amicable solution on their own, it seemed to get under my skin so fast. It's like I would be the sweetest, most attentive mum, and once they started arguing, I turned into the most decisive parent ever. I had no patience with it. I wanted to know who did what and bring resolve as fast as possible. After having had endless conversations with other parents, I've found it seems to be a universal reaction, including the mystery of how our own children seem to know which buttons to push when no one else on the planet ever could.

What I remember most when my patience wore thin with my girls was how that shift in emotion had the power to cloud my judgment. More than once I jumped to an understanding that wasn't altogether accurate. Because I wanted their arguing to stop first and foremost, I sometimes jumped to the wrong conclusion and offered up the wrong solution.

Have you ever found that to be the case? No wonder Solomon in all his God-inspired wisdom said that the first to state his case seems right. Nowhere has this been more obvious to me than when children tattle on one another! It took time, but with my girls, I learned to first gather all the facts before I rushed to judgment.

Imagine if we applied this practice to every area of our lives. If we exercised endurance and patience in gathering all the facts, taking them to God in prayer and giving Him as much time as He wants to show us the best decision. I'm years past refereeing little-girl spats, but I still lean into patience in all my decision-making. As you move through your day, why not do the same? Practice the endurance you have built internally. Lean into the patience you've developed in all your decision-making so you don't find yourself with cloudy judgment.

Heavenly Father, please help me not rush to judgment in all my decision-making, but help me to exercise patience in taking it all to You before I act. In Jesus' name, amen.

92 PATIENCE WITH TECHNOLOGY

Patience is better than power, and controlling one's emotions, than capturing a city.
PROVERBS 16:32

Not long after I learned I would get to climb Mount Whitney, Nick and the girls celebrated Mother's Day by giving me a Garmin watch. It was the perfect gift, and I couldn't have been more elated. I had been discussing how I needed to track my progress as I trained for my big climb, and my new gadget was the answer. Through the years, keeping up with my fitness with some kind of system had always been an effective way to stay motivated and on track—and by far, climbing Mount Whitney would be the biggest goal yet. A smart watch designed specifically for this upcoming climb would give me precise information and help me push myself as hard as I needed to and build more endurance.

The next day, when I began reading the instructions and doing exactly as they said, I couldn't get it to work correctly. I reread the instructions and repeatedly checked all the settings, to no avail. As my frustration mounted, I let out a big sigh, the kind that has a guttural sound with it, just for an added exhale of stress. As much as I wanted to start using it, I just couldn't spend another minute trying to figure it out. I imagine we all love technology until the moment we don't, and when it happens to me with my laptop, my phone, or smart watch, it can undo me. It's no surprise that I don't like to be slowed down. I suppose if I were more technologically savvy I wouldn't get so agitated, but it's not my greatest strength. I'm so grateful my girls can figure anything out and often come to my rescue. Once they teach me how to do something, I can usually move forward, but they were nowhere around to help.

Shouting to no one in particular, since I thought I was in the house alone, I shoved it back in the box and started walking away. About that time, Nick appeared from the hallway and, true to form, calmly picked up the watch and offered to show me what to do. He was very kind and patient, but the way I learn is very different from the way Nick does, and his way of giving a technology tutorial is more than I can take in one sitting. I just don't have the patience for it; yet patience is exactly what I need in every single one of the moments in life that try my patience. No wonder Proverbs says it's better than power, and that controlling our emotions is better than capturing a city!

Have you ever considered how many times in a single day you need patience? Anything can push us over the edge, can't it? A toddler. Traffic. Opening a pack of gum. Waiting in line for a fast-food order. The list is endless. Clearly, we'll never reach a place where we don't need to develop more patience, so let's embrace every one of the moments that come our way, even the times it involves a new gadget and more technology!

Father, please help me reframe the moments that try my patience so I can see them as opportunities to grow. I want to develop patience in the small things so I will have it for the big things. In Jesus' name. amen.

93 GOD IS PATIENT

A person's heart plans his way, but the LORD determines his steps.
PROVERBS 16:9

When I gave birth to Sophia, I was forty, and let me just say, if you pop out a kid at forty, I think you deserve a purple heart. From what I gather after talking to mothers around the globe, the sooner you have children, perhaps when you're younger and quite possibly more elastic, the sooner you might bounce back. The only problem with that suggestion in my life is that during the decade when I was younger and theoretically more elastic, Nick was nowhere to be found. So, according to God's plan for me, it wasn't until I was in my thirties that I became a mother—first with Catherine and then with Sophia.

A few weeks after Sophia was born, whatever elasticity I had, well, that's what I had to work with, and I was determined to get back into shape as quickly as possible. I remember enlisting the help of a trainer, fully expecting everything to just snap back into place in no time. Anxious to get moving, I even designed a six-week fitness program to help me jump back into my pre-pregnancy jeans. Remember, this was long before everyone wore leggings!

I'll never forget when the trainer showed up for the first time and listened to all my grand plans. Instead of being impressed and eager to join me in my enthusiasm, she laughed. Thinking she didn't understand me, I debated to myself whether I should repeat it. What could she possibly have not understood?

Being a far more patient person than me at the time, she pulled out a mat and asked me to lie down on my back. A bit bewildered, I followed her instructions, but I couldn't help wondering why we weren't getting started. It was then she began to help me understand that my body had a core group of muscles, ones that had been affected by having a C-section, and that my plan was premature. Instead, I needed to be patient, give my body time to heal, and start by working on my core. Then we would tackle some of my ideas.

I soon realized that it was like everything else in life: there are things we need to do first, then second, then third, and eventually, whatever it was that we really wanted to do in the first place—like that plan or purpose God put in our heart to pursue. On our way to where we know God has told us to go, there will always be steps to take, spiritual muscles to strengthen, and endurance to build. If we'll yield to His process, if we'll walk in His patience, we'll get where we need to go—in His perfect timing. It's a lifelong lesson we continually walk out, but no matter how patient we are one day and not so patient the next, God is always patient with us. Keep this in mind as you grow today. Take it to heart that He has all the patience in the world with you. It is He who will determine your steps.

Father, thank You for having unlimited patience with me while I grow and develop in being patient myself. Help me endure in faith taking one step at a time. In Jesus' name, amen.

94 WILLINGLY PAY
THE PRICE

"Which of you, wanting to build a tower, doesn't first sit down and calculate the cost to see if he has enough to complete it?"

LUKE 14:28

It's no secret that I am an over-the-top fan of the Olympics. It never stops impressing me how each new generation continues to break records in most every sport. I am often amazed at the capacity of the human body to endure and press through to a new level of achievement over and over again. And my family is right there with me.

For every Olympics, we are glued to the media coverage of the world's top performers pushing their bodies beyond their own limitations—even when they think they have nothing left to give. We cheer with them. We cry with them. We jump up and down, screaming in our living room—and sometimes in the middle of an airport if that's where we are. It is profound and inspiring to watch young men and women on the medal stand as their national anthem is played. If I knew all the words to most of them, I would probably sing along!

Each Olympian has worked so hard to get there. I've read that the average Olympian trains for four hours a day at least 310 days a year for six years before succeeding. For gymnast Simone Biles, it was even more. Simone is the most decorated American gymnast of all time.[43] Before the 2016 Summer Olympics, she trained six hours a day, six to seven days a week. Before the Olympics in Tokyo in 2021, she pushed it to seven hours a day.[44] On a personal level, she overcame being in and out of foster homes before she and her siblings were separated and adopted by her grandparents and extended family.

I'd say she paid the price. She has built endurance. She has exercised patience. She has done the hard work to get where she believes she's to go, where she wants to go.

I realize that most of us are not headed for Olympic-level competition, but I dare to believe we all want to achieve whatever is in God's heart for us to achieve, and it's no secret that we will have to pay some kind of price.

Paying the price means we will continue sacrificing to keep living a life of faith. We will continue being willing to work. We will continue being willing to endure patiently, moving forward for as long as it takes, to be all that God's created us to be, to do all that God's created us to do. To live purposeful. Intentional. On mission.

Let this resonate in your heart and mind today. When you come up against obstacles, hurdles, and even setbacks, be prepared to do whatever it takes, what maybe others are not willing to do, in order to fulfill your purpose. Willingly pay the price.

Heavenly Father, please help me have this kind of strength and endurance. Help me stay patient and focused on all that You've called me to be and do. In Jesus' name, amen.

95 PLUG INTO JESUS

A hot-tempered person stirs up conflict, but one slow to anger calms strife.

PROVERBS 15:18

It's incredible to think that we are the first generation to have all our communication, entertainment, news, and information literally in our hands. But when that world we hold in our hands runs out of power, most everything in our world comes to a screeching halt, doesn't it? One of the most interesting sights I've often seen is people running around in an airport with their chargers in their hands looking for an outlet. I've watched them pass by me, saying to no one in particular, "I need to plug my phone in. Where's the charging station? I need power. Does anyone know where I can plug my phone in? I have emails to answer." And on they will go. It's hilarious to listen to people having entire conversations with themselves, especially since I'm just as guilty and can totally relate. Although I might not be found talking about charging my phone, I am definitely one of those people who talks to themselves.

While watching people desperately searching for an outlet provides a bit of distraction while I'm waiting on flights, I think we're all like that at one time or another when it comes to our spiritual lives. We can get so busy with the demands of our lives that we let our spiritual batteries run too low. Then we inadvertently find ourselves running around, operating at about 1 percent, desperately in need of a charge.

But, unlike the free charging stations in the airports, there's a price to pay when we let our spiritual batteries drain dry. Today's verse gives us a glimpse of what can happen when we run low on power: It's all too easy to find ourselves hot under the collar, easily bothered by people who irritate us, or affected by circumstances that put us under pressure. We can find our patience wearing so thin that we grow a little hot-tempered, even about things we normally wouldn't. That's when we sometimes react in ways we never imagined or say what we live to regret. None of us wants to get into such a state, but it seems a natural consequence when we neglect to stay plugged into Jesus, when we don't stay connected to our true source of power, the One who can temper our natural tendencies.

When we stay plugged in and connected to Jesus, I find that we have less of a temper and more patience. We have more strength to bring calm to our world—and especially to our own hearts.

There's bound to be plenty to stir us up today and spark our tempers. Let's make a conscious effort to be slow to anger and to stay calm in every situation. To let those moments build endurance and patience in us so we can move forward in strength, being and doing all that God has created us to be and do.

Heavenly Father, please help me be slow to anger and full of patience so I can bring Your calming presence into every situation. You are my peace. In Jesus' name, amen.

96 SO YOU WON'T
BE SHAKEN

He will never be shaken. The righteous one will be remembered forever. He will not fear bad news; his heart is confident, trusting in the Lord.

PSALM 112:6–7

I was just eighteen when my mum told me that my dad had cancer. I remember not wanting to believe it, not wanting to face it, not wanting him to suffer through it. But none of my feelings had the power to stop what we all experienced as a family for the next several months. Together, we witnessed firsthand how cancer—not to mention chemo and radiation therapy—consumes a healthy body. We watched my dad go from a strong, independent man to a weak, frail one. We watched his beautiful thick black hair fall out of his head. We watched his strong frame slowly diminish to skin and bones. If you've lived through this with someone you deeply love, or have experienced it for yourself, you fully understand this kind of heartache.

When my dad could no longer drive, I drove him to his appointments. I sat in waiting rooms while he was in surgery. I learned what a financial burden endless treatments can be. And I watched my mum have a kind of patience that I had never seen her have before. There was a steadiness required of her, one she embraced with such fortitude and grace.

Though I had no way of knowing at the time, she had suffered before, long before I came along. As a teenage girl she and her sister had fled Egypt because of political instability and traveled forty days on a ship to Australia. In Sydney, she worked three jobs to save the fare for her parents and brother to join them. Maybe part of her patience was forged then. Once she and my dad married, she tried for years to have children and couldn't—another trying season when patience would have been necessary.

Like what happened in my family, life throws things our way that demand we move through them slowly and oftentimes painfully, developing a kind of patience we've never known or never had to lean into. A kind of patience that far surpasses waiting in lines, or listening to a long-winded storyteller, or steadying ourselves from getting short with someone struggling to count our change at the checkout. A kind of patience that reveals a strength in us we didn't know we had. In the quiet moments we know it can only come from God, but in the flurry of crisis we just tap into it and do what we have to do.

Maybe you're in such a place—one that requires a long-term kind of steady patience and endurance. Maybe you're a forever parent, a full-time caregiver, or someone battling your own illness. When you can catch your breath, lean into the Holy Spirit. Let His patience be your strength today. Keep trusting in the Lord so you won't be shaken, so your heart won't fear bad news. After all, He will never forget you and He's always with you.

Heavenly Father, please help me put my trust in You continually so I won't be shaken, so I won't fear bad news. Please help me walk in Your steady patience. In Jesus' name, amen.

97 EXTRAORDINARY PATIENCE

I received mercy for this reason, so that in me, the worst of them, Christ Jesus might demonstrate his extraordinary patience as an example to those who would believe in him for eternal life.

1 TIMOTHY 1:16

After almost a year of my dad battling cancer, my mother, brothers, and I were elated to finally hear the doctors use the word *remission*. We thought we were in the clear. The relief was indescribable. It had been such a long time since we had any expectation of normal. But then, just two weeks later, the unexpected happened. I raced home from work when Mum sent for me. The ambulance was parked outside our house, and a crowd of neighbors had gathered on our lawn. I walked in the front door to see my mum holding my dad's head in her lap. She had been helping him put on his shirt when he'd passed away.

I've never been able to unsee that moment. I've never been able to unfeel that shock and heartbreak. And while I'd love to be able to say I handled it well, I didn't, as I had no idea how to handle anything well back then. I was just starting to adult, as we say, and his death triggered a downward spiral in my life that I didn't know how to stop. I didn't know how to process my grief, so, like most people, I tried to numb it. I did what I could to not feel the loss, the pain, or the heartache.

The grief that unfolded in the following months was devastating for us all. I saw my distraught brothers try to process life without their hero. I saw my mum, who was normally a pillar of strength, become almost nonfunctional. She and my dad deeply loved each other, and I don't think she ever imagined life without him.

Maybe you've known such loss and confusion. Such heartache and chaos. Such highs and lows and then the lowest. Maybe you're there now. Maybe you're leaning into God with all your strength, enduring as best you can. But if you aren't sure how to, if you're afraid to, if it's been a while, I want to assure you that you are not alone. I know from experience that even when we don't know much about God, or we're not in touch with God, or we have more emotions than we know how to sort, He is more than patient with us. He truly understands and is for us, still. We're never beyond His mercy or His grasp.

I see this in the scripture when Paul wrote to Timothy and said that Jesus demonstrated extraordinary patience toward him. That's the kind of patience Jesus demonstrates toward us as well, no matter what we're going through. No matter how we might act out. No matter if we aren't sure what to pray, how to pray, or when to pray. He is patient with every single one of us through it all. Remember this as you move through your day. You can never get beyond His reach, and I feel sure He's reaching for you now.

Heavenly Father, please be with me in all the things I face and that I'm not sure how to manage. I don't understand everything that is happening, but I put my trust in You. In Jesus' name, amen.

98 HIS PERSPECTIVE
AND HIS PATIENCE

A person's insight gives him patience, and his virtue is to overlook an offense.
PROVERBS 19:11

K nocking on Catherine's bedroom door and opening it at the same time, I launched into my morning announcement before heading back downstairs: "Catherine, please bring your laundry downstairs so I can start the wash. Come on, get up, get moving. The sun's been up for quite a while now. Hurry up. Come on now."

The year before Catherine left for college, opening her bedroom door long after her alarm had gone off, surveying the laundry strewn across her floor, and reminding her to gather it up and get it downstairs to the laundry room became a daily ritual that agitated me more and more. If you have a teen, or an almost-not-a-teen, then I feel sure you get it. I wanted her to be ready to go off to school and be responsible, mature, and self-sufficient. And for some reason, despite all the ways she'd grown to be exactly what I had hoped, clothes on her bedroom floor hid all that from me. In fact, some days that was all I could see. Perhaps it was because I'm such an organized person, or maybe it's just because I'm a mother, and mothers like things in their home done a certain way. Or maybe it was because I was going to miss her terribly and I had no frame of reference for what to do with all the emotions of letting her go. Nick and I had spent more than one date night talking about it and tearing up.

We'd raised our girls traveling in ministry with us. We were the band! How could we be split up?

I'm sure you're laughing, especially if you've already been through one leaving the nest, but this was my first, and I was waffling between enduring in faith one day and being an absolute mess the next.

Waiting in the laundry room, I heaved a big sigh and headed back up the stairs. This time I didn't knock. I didn't ask her to gather up her clothes. I just started picking them up. I'll never forget the moment the Holy Spirit arrested me as I raced back down the steps. In a flash, His thoughts flooded my mind and I had to stop and thank God that I had a messy daughter upstairs lying in the bed, groggy with sleep, her floor covered in dirty clothes. I needed to think about all the mothers who would give anything to be in my shoes. Who would give anything to have another day with their son or daughter who was taken from them way too soon. Right there on the stairs, I began to pray for all those mothers.

Have you ever had God change your perspective like that? It's amazing how fast we can shift, isn't it? It's just like today's verse tells us: "A person's insight gives him patience." With God's insight, I instantly had more patience than before—and more compassion. As you move through today, let God's perspective give you fresh insight, the kind that leads to His perspective and His patience.

Heavenly Father, please flood my thoughts with Your perspectives. Help me see situations and circumstances through Your eyes. Help me live with patience. In Jesus' name, amen.

99 HIS HAND OF PROTECTION

The LORD will protect you from all harm; he will protect your life. The LORD will protect your coming and going both now and forever.

PSALM 121:7–8

L adies and gentlemen, we've arrived in Chicago a little earlier than planned so we will be waiting in the penalty box until the gate opens up in about thirty minutes."

While I appreciated the captain's sense of humor and sports reference, my ears heard it this way: "Mrs. Caine, while we know you have a connecting flight to make, and you are weary from having flown four days in a row, and you probably don't want to run through yet another airport and are desperate to get home and crawl into your own bed, under your own sheets, you will have to wait a little longer. Actually, much longer than expected. In fact, you will have to exercise patience for another twenty-four hours, if not for the rest of your life."

That is a bit dramatic, I know, but it's precisely how I feel when I hear someone—anyone—tell me something is going to take longer than planned, especially when I'm on an airplane or waiting in an airport—which I feel sure is where I've spent at least half my life! Can you imagine all the things I've said to God throughout the years? All the times I've pointed out to Him how long things were taking? When I just wanted to get from point A to point B? I'm so grateful God is patient, especially when I am not.

And yet, after all these years of waiting on tarmacs and in terminals, I have come to appreciate the protective hand of God on my life. I've learned to endure in faith and trust God's timing above weather delays, mechanical issues, or the late arrival of a crew to fly me the next leg of my journey. I don't want to be 35,000 feet in the air in the middle of a storm. I don't want a mechanical issue to force an emergency landing. I don't want an exhausted crew who are stressed to be responsible for my life and everyone else's on board. So I have learned to sit tight and trust that there are things going on in the physical realm and the spiritual realm far greater than I understand, and those are meant to keep me and everyone else safe.

Have you ever been kept waiting and later realized it was for your good? Did you ever hesitate at a green light and a car came speeding past in front of you? Even when things have happened in my life that I didn't expect, didn't want, or didn't understand, I've often stopped to thank God that He was still with me in the midst of it. I've had to be patient and trust that even when I can't see it, He's still protecting me in ways I don't know.

As you step through your day, thank Him for His hand of protection. He's always with us in all our comings and goings, both now and forever.

Heavenly Father, please help me remember that You are always with me—that You are guiding me and protecting me, often in ways I cannot see. I put my trust in You. In Jesus' name, amen.

100 CHERISH THE GLIMPSES

Start a youth out on his way; even when he grows old he will not depart from it.

PROVERBS 22:6

Mum, I just want them to be okay. Do you think they'll be okay? I don't think they know Jesus. I want their hearts to be happy. I just keep trying to love them and help. I don't know what else I can do. I care. I really, really do."

Sitting at dinner, looking at my baby girl's sweet face, listening to her talk about two friends and her heart of compassion to help them through a hard time, I couldn't help but feel eternally grateful. On the inside I was so moved to realize Sophia was growing up in every way—physically, emotionally, mentally, and spiritually—and in the ways we had hoped. She was caring for others and for their circumstances, for their emotions, for their eternal souls. On the outside, I tried to act calm and not let my mothering emotions show.

I thought of all the years of taking her to church, wondering if she actually listened to anything being said, curious if any of it made an impact, patiently doing what the Scripture instructed Nick and I to do— "Start a youth out on his way; even when he grows old he will not depart from it." Of course, the version I memorized early on in my parenting journey said, "Train up a child in the way he should go."[45]

From the onset of raising our girls, Nick and I committed to doing all we could to cultivate in them a love for Jesus, for His church, and for all people made in His image. All their lives Nick has talked with them through age-appropriate devotions, faithfully. When they've run into obstacles, he's brought those devotions back up to help them learn how to apply the truth and principles of God's Word practically. Still, you can't help but wonder along the way if any of it ever sticks.

Nick and I have always prayed God's Word over our girls. We've clung to the promises for them, including today's verse. They've grown up hearing me personalize and pray verses over them. Perhaps that's why getting a glimpse of the fruit in Sophia fuels me to keep watering even when I don't think anything is happening, because the truth is, God is always working—although I do wish He would show me glimpses more often.

If you're a parent, guardian, grandparent, or other devoted Christ-follower who is doing your best to ensure that the next generation knows Jesus, keep walking in patience. Keep enduring in faith. Keep pouring into their lives. Don't stop; and cherish the glimpses when they come, giving God all the glory.

Heavenly Father, please help me keep patiently watering the soil of the next generation's hearts. Help me pray, speak, and live, enduring in faith for them. In Jesus' name, amen.

NOTES

1. Matthew 25:23.
2. 2 Timothy 4:7.
3. Hebrews 10:36 ESV.
4. Merriam-Webster, s.v. "endurance," https://www.merriam-webster.com/dictionary/endurance.
5. J. Strong, *A Concise Dictionary of the Words in the Greek Testament and the Hebrew Bible* (Bellingham, WA: Logos Bible Software, 2009), 1:74.
6. 1 John 3:2.
7. Romans 8:11.
8. Philippians 4:13.
9. "The National Animals of Australia," WorldAtlas, https://www.worldatlas.com/articles/the-national-animals-of-australia.html.
10. Merriam-Webster, s.v. "learn," https://www.merriam-webster.com/dictionary/learn.
11. Philippians 3:13–14.
12. G. W. Parsons, "Humility," in *Evangelical Dictionary of Biblical Theology*, electronic ed. (Grand Rapids: Baker Book House, 1996), 361.
13. 2 Kings 7:5–10.
14. "Greek Verb Tenses (Intermediate Discussion)," http://ntgreek.org/learn_nt_greek/inter-tense.htm; and "Mark 8:27-38," Lectionary Greek, September 8, 2009, https://lectionarygreek.blogspot.com/2009/09/mark-827-38.html.
15. Ruth Harms Calkin, "My God Is So Big, So Strong, and So Mighty," 1959, public domain.
16. Andrea Thompson, "Your Odor: Unique as a Fingerprint," LiveScience, November 5, 2008, https://www.livescience.com/5188-odor-unique-fingerprint.html.
17. Galatians 5:22–23.
18. 2 Corinthians 5:17, 21; Romans 8:37.
19. Merriam-Webster, s.v. "dwell," https://www.merriam-webster.com/dictionary/dwell.
20. 2 Timothy 1:7 NKJV.

21. W. Arndt, F. W. Danker, W. Bauer, and F. W. Gingrich, *A Greek-English Lexicon of the New Testament and Other Early Christian Literature*, 3rd ed. (Chicago: University of Chicago Press, 2000), 640.
22. 1 Corinthians 2:16.
23. Philippians 4:11–14 AMPC.
24. "Battle of Marathon," History.com, https://www.history.com/topics/ancient-history/battle-of-marathon.
25. Proverbs 29:18 KJV.
26. 2 Kings 2:11–14.
27. 1 Corinthians 9:27 AMPC.
28. Philippians 3:12 ESV.
29. "Athens 2004 Olympic Games," Britannica, accessed November 1, 2021, https://www.britannica.com/event/Athens-2004-Olympic-Games#ref1083080.
30. Acts 16:16–18.
31. Romans 8:31.
32. Judges 13:5.
33. Mark 5:25.
34. Mark 5:26.
35. Mark 5:29.
36. Mark 2:1–8.
37. Mark 2:8–12.
38. Merriam-Webster, s.v. "wait," accessed November 1, 2021, https://www.merriam-webster.com/dictionary/waiting.
39. Biblehub.com, s.v. "hupomoné," https://www.biblehub.com/greek/5281.htm.
40. John 15:16.
41. Merriam-Webster, s.v. "prune," accessed November 1, 2021, https://www.merriam-webster.com/dictionary/prune.
42. Mary Forgione, "How to Hike Mt. Whitney: Your Journey Begins with the Permit Lottery," *LA Times*, February 1, 2020, https://www.latimes.com/travel/story/2020-02-01/mt-whitney-hiking-permit-lottery-to-begin.

43. "Simone Biles," Team USA, https://www.teamusa.org/usa-gymnastics/athletes/Simone-Biles.

44. Samantha Wilson, "Simone Biles Reveals Her Insane 7-Hour Training Schedule for Olympics: I Get 'Down and Dirty,'" Hollywoodlife.com, April 23, 2021, citing *The Tonight Show*, April 22, 2021, https://hollywoodlife.com/2021/04/23/simone-biles-olympics-training-schedule.

45. Proverbs 22:6 NKJV.

ACKNOWLEDGMENTS

You, dear reader, were foremost in my heart and mind in every devotion. I hope every day's encouragement strengthened you and prepared you for what God has prepared for you. Thank you for embarking on this adventure with me.

For any book, it takes a team to help an author birth a vision. I am so grateful to God for every person who brought their gifts, talents, and passion to this series.

To Elizabeth Prestwood: Having you alongside me as a collaborative writer, reliving every hike with me, and then helping me capture and develop most every story of my life into devotions has made the writing journey as adventurous as all the trails combined. This is the seventh book project we have worked on, and there's many more to come. Forever grateful to and for you.

To Dawn Jackson: Thank you for asking me to go hiking. I had no idea what one *yes* would lead to, but I'm so glad for all the adventures that followed. You opened up a world to me I never knew existed. From the magnificent views to the laughs to the injuries to the terrifying snakes, there's no one who could have made such adventures so fulfilling. You are a friend of more than twenty years, and I am forever grateful.

To our fellow hikers: You made our trips deep, meaningful, and more than hilarious. Our conversations meant so much to me. I love you all . . . Kate Czechowicz, Hilary Holmes, Evelyn Valenzuela, Amanda-Paige Whittington, and Whitney Wood.

To my husband, Nick: It was you who ensured I had all the right equipment, who packed my daypack so many Saturdays, who made sure I had all the right power snacks to keep me going, who willingly drove me to trailheads and back home when I wasn't sure I'd have the strength to do it. Most of all, thank you for believing in me. I love you. More and more, as the years go by.

To my girls, Catherine and Sophia: You are the joy of my life. Watching you grow, take your next steps in life, and live the plans and purposes God has mapped out for you is like having a front-row seat to the best adventure story ever. I'm so glad I get to be your mum. Thank you for letting me tell so many of your adventures in this devotional. I love you both.

To Andrew Stoddard, Janet Talbert, Laura Minchew, Jennifer Gott, MacKenzie Howard, Kristen Parrish, Mandy Mullinix Wilson, Sabryna Lugge, Kristen Golden, and the whole team at Thomas Nelson: Thank you for having such vision for these devotions. I saw one book and you saw three. You poured your heart and soul into every phase of this project. I am so grateful for this amazing team.

To Matt Yates: Thank you for your unending support and encouragement. You are a gift to Nick and me.

To Katie Strandlund-Francois: It was because of your commitment that every phase of this project stayed on track and got introduced to the world—timely, creatively, and descriptively. Thank you *@laurieanneart*. The artwork for the covers is stunning.

To our A21, Propel, ZOE Church, and Equip & Empower teams, volunteers, partners, and supporters: Serving Jesus alongside you in every corner of our world is the greatest privilege and honor of my life. Let's keep doing this.

To my Lord and Savior, Jesus Christ: You are the reason I will not only run my race but finish my course. You are so worthy of my all.

ABOUT THE AUTHOR

Christine Caine is a speaker, activist, and bestselling author. She and her husband, Nick, founded the A21 Campaign, an anti-human trafficking organization. They also founded Propel Women, an initiative that is dedicated to coming alongside women all over the globe to activate their God-given purpose. You can tune into Christine's weekly podcast, Equip & Empower, or her TBN television program to be encouraged with the hope of Jesus wherever you are. To learn more about Christine, visit www.christinecaine.com.

ISBN: 978-0-310-45796-1

R *esilient Hope*, a 100-day devotional from bestselling author, speaker, and activist Christine Caine, offers inspiration and biblical truth to help you build the endurance you need to run your race, fulfill the purposes and plans God has for you, and stay on mission—even in the face of setbacks and disappointments.

 Thomas Nelson
Since 1798

AVAILABLE IN PRINT,
E-BOOK, AND AUDIO